The Yo-Yo Diaries

The Yo-Yo Diaries

Spinning Toward Truth

NANCY LEE BETHEA

RESOURCE *Publications* · Eugene, Oregon

THE YO-YO DIARIES
Spinning Toward Truth

Copyright © 2025 Nancy Lee Bethea. All rights reserved. Except for brief quotations in critical publications or reviews, no part of this book may be reproduced in any manner without prior written permission from the publisher. Write: Permissions, Wipf and Stock Publishers, 199 W. 8th Ave., Suite 3, Eugene, OR 97401.

Resource Publications
An Imprint of Wipf and Stock Publishers
199 W. 8th Ave., Suite 3
Eugene, OR 97401

www.wipfandstock.com

PAPERBACK ISBN: 979-8-3852-6237-3
HARDCOVER ISBN: 979-8-3852-6238-0
EBOOK ISBN: 979-8-3852-6239-7

10/21/25

This book is dedicated to Horace and Dorothy Smith, my parents, for showing me where to find Truth, Beauty, and Goodness.

"Three things cannot be long hidden: the sun, the moon, and the truth."
BUDDHA

"Rather than love, than money, than fame, give me truth."
HENRY DAVID THOREAU

"Even if you are a minority of one, the truth is the truth."
MAHATMA GANDHI

"In a time of deceit, telling the truth is a revolutionary act."
GEORGE ORWELL

Contents

List of Illustrations | ix

Acknowledgments | xi

    Journal Entry | 1

1   Challenges | 3

    Waiting Room | 5

    A Yellow Yo-Yo | 6

    Session One | 7

    What I Write with my Green Pen | 11

    Just a Test | 14

    Obstacles | 19

    Dr. Dey | 22

    Why? | 24

    Explaining Those Cs | 26

    Shedding Light on the Ps | 27

    Trevor | 29

    Another Yo-Yo | 31

    One Answer Key | 32

    The Conference Room—Part 1 | 34

    In Trouble for What? | 36

    The Conference Room—Part 2 | 37

    Reformed | 41

    The Conference Room—Part 3 | 42

Contents

    Trev | 45
    Airplanes | 49
    Grandpa | 51
    Meeting Odysseus | 52
    What I Would Say to Odysseus | 53
    Back to Therapy | 55

2 Changes | 57
    Flight to Daytona | 59
    Fly-Rony | 62
    The Yo-Yo Diaries Part 1: In-Flight Conversation with Myself | 63
    Airport Meetings | 65
    Mocha Cookie Crumbles | 67
    Coffee and Callie | 68
    Wanna Talk About It? | 71
    The Yo-Yo Diaries Part 2: My Side of the Table | 74
    The Books | 76
    My New Room with a View | 78
    Sunday Before Bed | 81
    Odysseus and Me | 83

3 Calliope | 85
    Calliope | 87
    Monday Morning | 88
    Cognitive Benefits of Writing—Part 1 | 90
    Helping Old People | 92
    A Happy Memory or Two | 95
    (Ugh! Forced rhymes yet again, but it's a rough draft) | 97
    Anxiety, Called Up Front | 98
    Sharing is Caring . . . Seriously? | 100
    Albert's Happy Memory—Flying Saucers | 102
    Who's Next? | 104

Contents

Toby | 105
On the Way Home | 106
Trev's Call | 107
Trev's Story | 109
Tuesday | 112
Life Experiences | 113
Experiencing Life | 115
Turn and Talk (Part 1) | 117
Cognitive Benefits of Writing (Part 2) | 118
Toby's Piece: Beautiful Bubbles | 119
Turn and Talk (Part 2) | 120
Driving Home on Tuesday | 122
The Yo-Yo Diaries Part 3: Writing Trues | 123
Callie's Note | 124
Wednesday's Prompt | 126
"What Do You Imagine Now?" | 128
Wednesday's Share Time | 130
Wednesday's Trip Home | 132
Books-A-Million on a Wednesday Evening | 134
Late Wednesday Night | 140
Thursday Morning | 142
Thursday's Session | 143
My Fears: A Brief History | 145
Writing Wrain? | 146
Share Time: Harold | 147
The Yo-Yo Diaries Part 4: Whose Truth? | 149
Toby Taps Me on the Shoulder and ... | 152
Identity | 153
Gran Takes Over | 154
Mom's Call | 156
Toby's Invitation | 158
Callie's Conversation | 159

Contents

4 Clearing | 161
Salt Water | 163
Part of Myself | 166
Maya's Call | 167
Friday Morning | 169
Where's Toby? | 170
Friday's Prompt | 171
The Yo-Yo Diaries Part 5: Hopes and Dreams | 173
Truth Doesn't Wait | 175
Another Phone Call! | 179
Pre-Flight | 182
Thoughts on My Flight Home | 184

5 Chances | 185
My Dad | 187
Arriving Home | 189
Chemo Conversation | 191
Saturday Morning | 194
In Trev's Room | 195
Mom Returns | 197
Side Effects | 198
Puzzles | 199
Hospitals | 200
Parents at . . . Peace? | 201
The Café with my Father | 203
Monday at School | 206
Morning Pages | 209
Called Out of Biology | 211
Dr. Dey's Conference Room | 212
Using My Voice | 214
Dr. Dey | 216
Back in Biology Class | 221

Contents

Driving Home | 223
Changes | 225
Another Office Conference? | 227
Maya's Truth | 229
Gran is Here! | 232
Outside Dr. Dey's Office | 234
Who Are These People? | 240
The Yo-Yo Diaries Part 6: Trev's Condition | 241
Morning Pages | 242
Last Week of School | 243
Airborne | 244
Repeat | 246
Joy! | 248
Gran's Poem | 249
Toby's Poem | 250
Restful | 251
A Visit from Callie | 253
Reunion | 255
My Poem: Circles | 257
Published! | 259
Opposites Attract? | 261
A New Year | 262

Epilogue | 265

Truth Seeker | 267
Journal Prompts Recommended by Bloom | 269

List of Illustrations

Figure 1 - Amalee Rivera | ii

Figure 2 – Alexandria Masters | 3

Figure 3 – Carly Shannon | 57

Figure 4 – Jasmyn Joseph | 85

Figure 5 – Ivy Peterson | 161

Figure 6 – Sasha Bass | 185

Figure 7 – Kylie McCarthy | 265

Acknowledgments

Writing this book has truly been a labor of love. When I outlined it, I never dreamed it would morph into what it is today. For that, I thank my creative writing students at LaVilla School of the Arts in Jacksonville, Florida. Every day, they show me that creativity is alive and well in the younger generation.

In addition, I must thank Ms. Nicole Defeo's visual arts students at LaVilla School of the Arts for drawing the yo-yos used in this book.

I'd also like to thank my mom, Dorothy Smith, for reading every draft and for making spot-on suggestions to tighten the writing. I appreciate the insightful suggestions on characterization offered by my sister, Stephanie Guthrie.

My husband, Stan, offered unwavering support and formatting help (even while he battled cancer) throughout the writing of this book. Additionally, I thank my daughter, Hayden, for unknowingly inspiring many parts of this book.

Last but not least, I must thank Calliope "Callie," the Muse of Epic Poetry, for her creative inspiration.

From Bloom's Lace Journal

Wednesday, August 13

JOURNAL ENTRY

Just pulled out last year's journal, the one I got from Tessa's office. Am I ready for this? Maybe.

Nowadays, I realize I was in an ocean with tides going in and out, up and down, and unseen undercurrents underneath. Or, maybe that's just what all freshmen go through.

Back then, I wrote everything in poetry. Why, oh, why?! Rhyme Queen of Red Hills High, right here!

A new school year starts tomorrow. Another yo-yo year as a sophomore? Four honors academics, a humanities class, a creative writing class (yay!), and French 1. Guess who's in all four of my honors classes!

Yep, Mara!

Still not sure why she did it. How could anyone be jealous of me?

Anyways, here goes...

1

Challenges

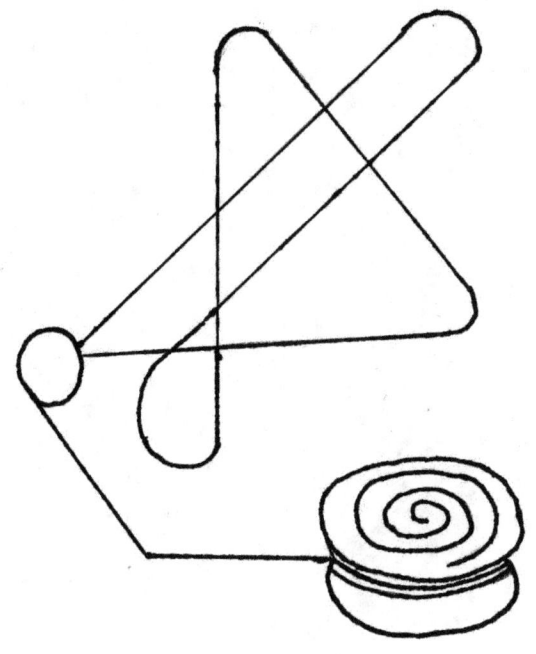

Family Counseling Services—Atlanta, Georgia
TUESDAY, APRIL 2

WAITING ROOM

I'm open to this idea, I guess.
Feels like a monumental game of chess.

I retreated, stopped talking so much,
The parentals decided I had anxiety and such.

Currently, I'm undecided,
Or just young and unguided.

I sit in a waiting room,
Not sure what's awaits. Relief or doom?

I've never been to "therapy"
Will it offer a remedy?

I think they're gonna make me talk
Tell me I have some kind of block.

I'm just looking for something real and true,
Perhaps "therapy" will give me a clue.

Family Counseling Services—Atlanta, Georgia
Tuesday, April 2

A YELLOW YO-YO

The basket beside my chair
Holds toys, puzzles, small stuffed bears.

I dig through it as I wait
The items? I don't love or hate.

But then, I see a yellow disc
Picking it up feels like a risk.

It's a yo-yo, bright as the sun.
Been a while since I played with one.

Around my finger, I wrap its string,
And then, this yo-yo sprouts wings!

Up and down, and all around
A giggle from my mouth sounds.

My grandpa taught me how to throw,
And do tricks with a yellow yo-yo.

Rock that Baby and Walk the Dog
Slowly, I emerge from my fog.

Down and up, and up and down
This yo-yo reverses my frown.

Family Counseling Services—Atlanta, Georgia
Tuesday, April 2

SESSION ONE

I feel better after playing with the yo-yo,
I've calmed down,
Even though Mom dropped me off here,
And I had to check in
By myself.
Because she is "running errands."

Now, I sit in the waiting room.
But what am I *waiting* for?

To go into another room
And talk, I guess.

Just talk?

Talking is overrated,
So advocated.

I would rather write.

A door opens
And a young woman with long curly hair smiles.
She holds a file folder and a tablet computer.

"Chloe?"

I nod.

"Right this way."

She leads me through a maze of offices
Until we reach one near the back.

I like it.

Varying shades of brown and beige.
Lots of books, comfy couches,
Colored pencils, paper.

Fresh journals, colored pens?
Be still my heart!
A Keurig!

She shuts the door
And smiles again.

"I'm Tessa.
Want a hot chocolate or a chai tea?"

"Yes, please."
I run my finger over the K-Cup choices,
Selecting a chai tea.

She sits in an oversized chair
And opens a file folder.

The Keurig sputters.
Water falls into my cup.

I see a variety of sweeteners-
Honey, Truvia, Sugar, and Molasses.
I pick up the Honey Bear,
For some reason, I want to hug it,
Maybe I want the Honey Bear to hug me.
I spoon the thick golden sweetness into my cup,
Stir it in,
Wrap my hands around its warmth,
And carry my cup to the other comfy chair
And sit.

"So, I see here you go by Bloom.
That's a nice name," Tessa says.

"My grandfather told me Chloe means 'blooming' in Greek
Or something, so he started calling me Bloom when I was a baby.
It just stuck."

She nods and writes something down.

I take a sip of my tea,
Warm peace fills my mouth.
My eyes rest on the stack of journals.

"Want to write?" Tessa asks.

I quickly say yes, surprising myself.

"Go ahead.
I'll write too."

I set down my tea,
Walk to the table,
Pick up a new blue journal and a green pen.

At home, I usually write in my old composition book,
The one I got in middle school,
And any pen or pencil I can find.

I sit again,
In the oversized, comfy chair
Opposite Tessa,
And I write.

From Bloom's Blue Journal
Tuesday, April 2

WHAT I WRITE WITH MY GREEN PEN

I guess I have an ideal life.
No unmet needs, only a little strife,

From the outside, looking in.

But, from my perspective, from my eyes,
You would see many half-truths, even lies.

I'm only 14, after all,
And I have to figure out this squall . . .

Of wind and rain, my own hurricane.

My parents? By all accounts successful.
To me, however, they're somewhat neglectful.

They work *all the time,*
Up the ladder, they continually climb.

Dad's a pilot with a big airline,
Mom's in demand for interior design.

He's of Jamaican and English descent,
She's a Southern White gal with an accent.

Opposites attract? Really?!?

We live in a suburban three-story
With a manicured lawn and front porch glory.

There's so much pressure about school
For me, honors classes rule!

I have a little brother, love him so.
He's been sick, we can't go outside and throw.

So ...

Here I am
At "Family Counseling Services"
With Tessa.

Will she be the one to "heal" me?
The key to unlock a strategy
That sets my voice free?

"How's it going?" Tessa asks.

Do I nod and keep writing,
Or stop and agree to a chat?

"Can I read you what I wrote," Tessa asks.

Wait, what?
She wrote too?

Maybe I won't die here
Not yet anyway. I won't sneer.

"I have a big test tomorrow," I tell her.

Where did that come from?
Why am I sharing?

"Want to talk about it?" she asks.
"No pressure, just a little small talk," she adds.

I tell her about the big state writing test
At school tomorrow.

Red Hills High School Cafeteria—Atlanta, Georgia
WEDNESDAY, APRIL 3

JUST A TEST

"It's just a test," Mom said.
"Do your best."

But Mom hasn't spent two solid hours
Seated at a lunch table,
Hunched over a laptop.
Having her literacy evaluated lately, now has she?

Is it really just a test, Mom?

This test
Determines class placement for next year
Which
Decides the colleges I apply for
Which
Designates the job I land
Which
Dictates the life I live,

According to you, Mom!

You're the one who will drool
Over my test results from school
Because with you, scores rule!

But then, the bell rings.

"Good morning, Red Hills High," the student announcer says.
"Please stand for the Pledge of Allegiance."

It's almost Test Time.

"I pledge allegiance ... "

My hands moisten.

"To the flag ... "

The seismic shift in my abdomen
Reminds me I had only a Pop Tart for breakfast,
Now, it's a frosted strawberry serpent slithering in my stomach.

"Of the United States of America."

The cafeteria door opens.
I look at our proctor,
Mr. Robertson, who frowns
Because someone is late
Entering this "testing room,"
a.k.a. the cafeteria.

Please be Maya.
Please be Maya.

The moving student stops beside me.
Maya Cross, my best friend since sixth grade,
Places her backpack on the table
And sighs.

"And to the republic,"

Maya pulls out her
School-issued laptop.

"For which it stands."

I risk a tiny wave.
She nods.

"One nation under God"

Mr. Robertson makes a no phone motion
With his hands
And waits . . .

"Indivisible,"

. . . For Maya to power down her cell phone
And zip it into a front pocket
Of her backpack.

"With liberty and justice for all."

Mr. Robertson watches as Maya carries her backpack
Into the hallway,
Placing it on the floor
With all the other canvas slaves
That will wait while their student masters
Take yet another test.

"Good morning, students,"
Our principal, Dr. Dey says.
"We expect the best from you today
On your state writing test.
Good luck, Mustangs!"

I watch Maya come back in
And find her assigned testing seat.

"You'll do great," she whispers
And fist bumps me as she passes.

She's cheerful.

Mr. Robertson clears his throat,
Slides his glasses closer to his eyes,
And reads his "official" test administration script.

"Today, you will complete the writing portion
of the State Assessment Test.
You will be given a prompt
and exactly 120 minutes to read the prompt,
write your response,
and revise your piece.
Please use your time wisely."

More words and more words.
Two warnings about cell phones,
Smartwatches, and all the other
Electronics that help people cheat.

Finally, we login to our laptops,
Click on some final warning about plagiarism,
and start the test.

I read the prompt
and smile.

Red Hills High School Cafeteria—Atlanta, Georgia
WEDNESDAY, APRIL 3

OBSTACLES

I love writing
Because it relaxes me.

I relish writing in my new blue journal,
Feeling my pen glide on the paper
Like a figure skater on ice.

But today, that's not possible.

I don't hate writing on a computer,
It just feels artificial.
The computer is an intruder between
My thoughts and the words I write.

At least they gave us scratch paper.

I re-read the prompt for the fourth time:
"Obstacles are a part of life. It's how people face them that matters.
In an organized, logical essay, discuss the obstacles you, someone you know, or someone you have read about overcomes obstacles in life. Be sure to give detailed examples to support your conclusions."

I'm halfway through my essay,
Beginning paragraph four now.

My eyes itch.
It feels like that sugar rub
Mom uses on her hands
Coated my eyes.

"Students, please stop working
And close your laptops," Mr. Robertson says.

Wait!
I check the time.
We still have 67 minutes.
I'm not finished!
I just wrote about Odysseus overcoming the Sirens
By plugging his soldiers' ears with beeswax.

Mr. Robertson repeats himself.
I don't want to stop writing,
But I close my laptop anyway.

I like Mr. Robertson.
He's my English teacher.
And, he's a C in my book.
(I wrote about the Cs and the Ps in my blue journal),
But, his face is stern, fretful.

The cafeteria doors open.
Dr. Dey enters,
Flanked by two men wearing dress shirts, coats, and ties.

This, really?
Such drama!

Dr. Dey is definitely a P.
But the Ties?
Who are they?
Grammar police?
Essay graders?
Here to arrest the comma criminals among us?

I chuckle.
Maya looks at me.
She's smirking too.

"Students, please leave your computers on the tables.
We are all moving outside for a few minutes," Dr. Dey says.

Outside, under a gray Georgia sky.
The cool April air startles me.
I just want to finish my essay.

I hope it saved.
I really like what I wrote.

Outside Red Hills High School Cafeteria—Atlanta, Georgia
Wednesday, April 3

DR. DEY

We stand under a quilt of silver clouds.

Still in testing mode,
We can't talk
Or communicate *in any way.*

Dr. Dey's yellow suit
Daubs the muted scene
With some color.

The Ties stand near the cafeteria doors,
Securing the school?
Or us?
Or the laptops?
Yep, they're probably here
For the laptops!

Dr. Dey and Mr. Robertson walk toward me.

Me?

"Chloe Howard?" Dr. Dey says.
"Please come with me,
And please gather your computer
And all your test materials
From the cafeteria."

She uses my legal name.
Doesn't she know I go by Bloom?

Maya shrugs as I pass her.

I look for assurance
From Mr. Robertson,
But his eyes are cold pewter,
Reflecting the sunless sky.

I feel like I'm being taken to jail.

Maybe *I* am the comma criminal.

Red Hills High School Main Office—Atlanta, Georgia
WEDNESDAY, APRIL 3

WHY?

I don't think I'm in trouble.

Mr. Robertson did in fact *give* us peppermint candies
During the test.
Which is probably against some district rule,
But hasn't peppermint candy been shown enhance brain function
Or something?

Dr. Dey's bracelets jingle as
She motions me
Through the door
Of her office.

"Have a seat, Chloe."

My stomach twists again.
I feel like one of those long balloons
being curled into a dog or a seahorse
By a balloon artist
At the County Fair.

I sit.

I notice a painting of sunflowers behind her desk.
Touches of yellow everywhere.

Does the color mean caution?
Or optimism?
Or cowardice?

From Bloom's Blue Journal

EXPLAINING THOSE CS

The Creatives,
People who don't
Begin with the end in mind.

They welcome colors, shapes,
Sounds, smells, and tastes
To their inner and outer spaces.

They're open.
They listen.
They think, craft, make, dream, draw, write,
And live.

They're Creatives.

My brother Trev is a C.
Mr. Robertson is a C.

My dad?
No. Way. No. Way. No. Way.
He fills every moment with work!

My mom?
Hmmm.
Maybe back in 1996 she had a moment as a C.

Doubtful.

From Bloom's Blue Journal

SHEDDING LIGHT ON THE PS

The Practicals.

I admit,
Ps are needed in this world.

I mean, I don't want to spend all day pulling weeds,
Or fix the dryer when it overheats.
Mom is always washing clothes!

But, seriously.

My dad never relaxes.
Never.

It's like he has an inner voice
Commanding him to fill every moment
With work, jobs, tasks, toil, labor, travail, industry,
Struggle.
(I looked up some of those words in a thesaurus).

Even when our family watches a movie
He sits with an open laptop,
Working or researching or reading news feeds.
Can you even say relaxation, Dad?

Ps can be helpful, I suppose.

They come to your house
Ready to cook, to clean, to build.

But do Ps ever stop and gaze
At the sunset?
Or think great ideas,
Or write funny stories,
Or consider
What's
Really
True
In this world?

From Bloom's Blue Journal

TREVOR

He's six.
I'm 14.
He's the little brother I prayed for.

Annoying?
Yes, sometimes, but he makes me laugh.

He's all love,
With arms reaching toward me
When I walk in his room.
He wants to spend time with me.

"A bedtime story, Bloomie?
Please?" he asks every night,
Holding his books, his stuffed giraffe named Jeffy, and his blue blankie.

I want to tell him I've still got loads of Biology and History homework,
But I usually make another choice,
And we snuggle into the beanbag in his room,
And I read to him.
First, "A Pocket for Corduroy."
Then another book and another.
He falls asleep beside me.
I cover him
In the beanbag.

Kiss his cheek.
Return to my homework.

Tomorrow, he goes to the hospital
For tests.

And Friday, I go back to therapy.
Ugh!

The parentals think Trev has leukemia.
At six?
Is that even possible?

Does leukemia need Trev's love
Like I do?

From Bloom's Blue Journal

ANOTHER YO-YO

I bought a green
Yo-Yo
For Trev.

It glows in the dark.

I slid the string
Onto his finger,
But he's weak,
And, he dropped it.

It's going to take work,
To bring it back up
From all the downs,

But so many things do.

On the way to Atlanta Children's Hospital
Thursday, April 4

ONE ANSWER KEY

The purple morning light greets us
As we load into our SUV.

"Sit by me the whole way, Bloomie.
The whole way. Okay?" Trev pleads.

I packed Jeffy, ten of his favorite books,
His blanket, and a tablet.

The drive isn't too bad.

Mom slurps coffee, then sighs.

Dad, in his uber "P" mode,
Drives to the hospital through Atlanta traffic.

No words on the way,
But Trev and I snuggle.

We arrive and check in.

Trev's room has lots of natural light
And soft colors.

At least, he can relax here.

Photos of kids on playgrounds, shooting baskets, hiking mountain trails
Adorn the walls.

'Healthy kids are active kids,'
Is the message I receive loud and clear.

We know
He's here for more tests,
But I wonder what the doctors
Have already seen on
Trev's answer key.

I look out the room window,
Lavender light turns yellow
As the city awakens.
Does the yellow represent
My optimism or cowardice?

Dad drives me to school a little later,
Before heading to the airport for work.

I'm unsure what this day will bring.

Red Hills High School Main Office Conference Room—
Atlanta, Georgia
Thursday, April 4

THE CONFERENCE ROOM—PART 1

"Come on in, Chloe," Dr. Dey says.
I follow her past a painting of
Sunflowers hanging behind her desk.

We enter a conference room
With a rectangular table
Resting under cool fluorescent lights.

"Your mom will be here soon," she says.

She sits at one end of the table.
I sit in a chair on her left
And doodle in my blue journal.

She inhales, ready to speak,
But the door opens, and the two men in ties enter,
Followed by Ms. Kelly, the guidance counselor,
And, Mr. Robertson.

Ms. Kelly sits opposite me,
Mr. Robertson smiles and sits beside me.

The Ties stand in the back, conferring.

My mom enters,
Holding her ever-present cup of joe.
She sits by Ms. Kelly.

Whose side are you on, Mom?

Dr. Dey stands, closes the door.
"Let's begin."

The Ties sit opposite Dr. Dey.
Their gold "Department of Education"
Badges shine, pinned on their lapels.

So official
They've gotta be Ps.

From Bloom's Blue Journal

IN TROUBLE FOR WHAT?

In third grade,
I got in trouble for talking,

But it wasn't my fault.
I know everyone says that,
But it really wasn't.

Julia Rodriguez asked
To borrow my mechanical pencil
Because she was out of lead,
But I didn't hear her,
So I said,

"What did you say?"

I'm the one who got in trouble.
My clip moved from blue to yellow.

Does yellow still mean trouble?

Am I in trouble now?
I wish I knew what I did.

*Red Hills High School Main Office Conference Room—
Atlanta, Georgia*

Thursday, April 4

THE CONFERENCE ROOM—PART 2

Dr. Dey introduces everyone
Then asks Ms. Kelly to begin.

Her voice is strained, pinched,
Like stiff arms and legs
Attached to a body that hasn't stretched in months.

"Good morning.
Bloom is such a good student,
But on her state test this morning,
There was a problem."

My mom sips her coffee.
The furrow between her eyebrows deepens.
The residue of long hours in Trev's hospital room shows.
Now this.
I almost empathize . . .
For a moment.

"We think Chloe may have plagiarized," Dr. Dey adds.

I feel I'm floating above
The room,
Observing these people and their actions
From the sky.

Plagiarism?
Really?
Did they even read my essay?

"Our proctors," Dr. Dey pauses and nods to the Ties,
"Can monitor each student's test in real time."

She waits, looks down, brushes something off her yellow jacket.

"Chloe's essay was good. Too, too good."

She reaches into a file folder,
Pulls out papers.

"We've printed it here.
It's only partially finished."

Yep, but I wanted to finish!

Dr. Dey hands the paper to the Ties.

"Chloe included three references, *very specific references*
To 'The Odyssey' in her essay.
No 9th grader I know has read,
Actually read, Homer."

She laughs.
No one else joins her.

Could she be any more judgy?

"My dad read it to her
When she was little."
My mom says, voice grainy.
"More than once."

Dr. Dey looks at Mr. Robertson.
"Could Chloe could write this?" she asks him.

Mr. Robertson pauses,
Pushes his glasses closer to his eyes
As he examines my writing.
"Actually, yes."

He glances at me.
"She's an excellent writer.
We just entered one of Chloe's poems
In a national writing contest."

"This is obviously *not* a poem," Dr. Dey responds,
Her P glory shining bright.

Do I get to speak?
Do I want to speak?

"Bloom's test scores are consistently in the 90th percentile,"
Ms. Kelly adds, glancing in my file.
"Perhaps she could her deliver her essay orally
Or rewrite the essay in front of us?
It would prove what she knows."

The question is the cause
Of a very pregnant pause.

Mom speaks next.

"Bloom's written stories since she could hold a crayon," my mom says.
She puts her coffee cup on the table.
"Bloom wouldn't copy anyone's work,
She wouldn't need to."

"Well," Dr. Dey responds.
"I'll speak to the representatives
from the Department of Education about those options," she pauses.
"But for now, it's been ruled
Plagiarism."

The Ties nod but remain silent.

"Her test has been invalidated," Dr. Dey says.
"As is the normal course in test violations,
Chloe will be attending Atlanta Reform School
for a week."

Atlanta Reform School?
Do I need to be reformed?

From Bloom's Blue Journal

REFORMED

Lots of things
Need to be reformed.

Laws,
Like amendments to the Constitution,
The dent in the back bumper of our SUV,
Solids into liquids or gasses.

Am I a law
Or a car
Or a solid?

No, but when I think of Trev,
I break
Into a million
Tiny pieces,
That can't be
Reformed
Until
He
Gets
Better.

*Red Hills High School Main Office Conference Room—
Atlanta, Georgia*

Thursday, April 4 after lunch

THE CONFERENCE ROOM—PART 3

"Bloom's oral exam
Proved she knows quite a bit
About *The Odyssey,* but
Her test remains invalidated" Dr. Dey says.

"Do you have any proof?"
Mom asks.

Dr. Dey and Tie #1 exchange glances.

He nods.

Mom's eyes meet mine.
She's thinking.

"Dr. Dey . . . ," Mom asks.
"Would you consider an alternative?"

*Gotta give Mom credit.
She's bold.
Maybe I should try coffee.*

"Such as?" Dr. Dey responds.

Dr. Dey's dismissive tone
Descends upon the room
Like freezing rain.

"My mother is a retired school librarian.
She lives in Daytona Beach, Florida.
She just started a reading and writing program
With senior citizens in nursing homes.
They read books and discuss them,
and she's about to start writing with them.
I know she needs help
As she expands it."

Mom pauses.

"Could Bloom help there?
Her grandmother could verify her hours
And complete all the forms."

Daytona for a week?

"Would the school consider this instead of reform school?"
Mom pushes.
"We can fly her down. My husband's a pilot."

"As long as Chloe doesn't hang out
On the Daytona racetrack," Dr. Dey says with a laugh.

Nobody else joins in.

Ms. Kelly looks at me.
My face reddens.

"That's a highly unusual proposal," Dr. Dey continues.
"I'll talk it over
With our Georgia Department of Education representatives,
But I doubt they will consider it.
I'll also speak with Mr. Hayes, my assistant principal,
And appropriate district personnel,
Get their input.
Again, approval is highly unlikely," she pauses.
"In any case, we will put together some paperwork.
I'll have my secretary call you in the morning
With our final decision," Dr. Dey says.

She stands.
Ms. Kelly stands.
Mr. Robertson stands.
The Ties were already standing.
Mom stands.

I'm the last to stand.
"I'd like to do that," I say.

Atlanta Children's Hospital, Atlanta, Georgia
Thursday afternoon, April 4

TREV

The test results came back.
Trev has an aggressive form of leukemia.

The disease has increased,
But Trev has decreased,
He's smaller, reduced, shrunken,
Like one of his stuffed animals
Nestled down into the sheets.

I bought him a new blanket
In the gift shop.
It has different airplanes flying
In various directions.

I don't know why I picked this one.
I guess I am my dad's daughter.

"I'm going to Gran's for a week," I tell Trev.

Mom got the call from Dr. Dey this morning.

Trev squeezes Jeffy.

"I got you something," I say.

I unfold and spread
The airplane blanket over him,
Tucking it all around him
Like I do at home.

"You're the pilot, Trev,
Of all these planes."

I pause before speaking,
Trying to quell the emotion in my voice.

"You're going so many places
In the future."

"But you're leaving, Bloomie," Trev says.
His pure eyes pierce me
Before he pulls the blanket over his head.

"I'm going to help Gran
At the nursing home," I say.

"Who's gonna read to me?"
He asks, his voice muffled.

I smile and pull out a digital recorder.
It's the size of a small candy bar.

"I am, Trev."

A skinny arm reaches out from under the airplanes.

I hand the recorder to him.

He turns it on and pushes play.
My voice fills the room,
Stating the title and author of the first book . . .
"'Goodnight, Moon' by Margaret Wise Brown."

He smiles.
He listens.

He and recorded me say together,
"In the great green room."

He stops the recording.

"How many?"

"Twelve."

"Twelve is not enough," he says.
"Not enough. Not enough."

"Okay, fine," I respond.
"I'll record more."

"Promise?" he asks,
Popping his head out from the blanket and
Stretching his arms to me.

The tears release themselves
And journey down my face.

I hug him tight,
So tight.

"You're strong, Trev!
Be brave!"

He doesn't let go.

"Let's fly somewhere, Bloomie!"
He finally says.

I nod and ask,
"In which plane?"

He points at the 747 on the blanket.

"Where do you want to go?" I ask him.

"To Gran's
In Florida!" he yells.

"Tell you what.
I'll call you every night
While I'm at Gran's.
Maybe I'll even
Facetime you."

He nods and smiles
And hugs me tighter.

From Bloom's Blue Journal

AIRPLANES

I was a baby
The first time I flew.

I don't remember it.

Then, when I was six,
My parents put me on a plane
From Atlanta
To Daytona.

All. By. Myself.

Miss Laurie, a flight attendant,
Checked on me.
She and my dad worked on the same crew
Back then.

Miss Laurie gave me a bag of
Chips Ahoy cookies
And a bottle of milk.

Best. Snack. Ever.

She also gave me a LaLaLoopsy coloring book
And a fresh box of crayons.

She even colored with me.

Grandpa greeted me at the end of the walkway
From the plane.

He gave me a big hug
And thanked Miss Laurie.

That night, he started reading
The Odyssey
To me.

From Bloom's Blue Journal

GRANDPA

His voice, deep and resonant,
Always comforted me.

Safety, protection,
Peace.
A deep sigh.

Grandpa was a trial lawyer,
One of the best in
Florida,
I was told.

A year after I was born,
He retired
And read books all day long.

At least, that's what I thought.

What could be better?

From Bloom's Blue Journal

MEETING ODYSSEUS
(the first time)

Grandpa's library had over 3000 books,
Labeled and organized,
Cross-referenced by genre and subject
Thanks to Gran, ever the librarian.

I remember his voice, sunlight, ocean waves,
And meeting Odysseus.

I was six.

I sat beside him
On an oversized brown leather chair
With a crocheted blanket, a small stuffed purple monkey,
And the faint smell of pipe tobacco.

He read and read.

I listened and listened.

Sometimes, I sketched in a small notebook.

I still have that notebook.
I looked through it after his funeral.

From Bloom's Blue Journal

WHAT I WOULD SAY TO ODYSSEUS

I always thought you made things
Harder than they really were.

I wonder if I do the same thing.

Like concrete mix,
Drying.
You waited for situations to harden before you took action.

Is that stubbornness
Or a form of optimism?

I remember watching a crew spread concrete mix
On the driveway of our house
Before Trev was born.

I gazed from an upstairs window
For hours.

Pour and smooth.
Pour and smooth.

Now, the driveway to my heart
Is poured
And smoothed
And drying,

hardening,
becoming fixed,

Like concrete.

How can I soften it again?

Family Counseling Services
FRIDAY AFTERNOON, APRIL 5

BACK TO THERAPY

"I see you have your journal,"
Tessa says.

I nod and actually
Hold up my green pen.

"Can I get a chai tea?"

She nods, then asks,
"How'd your test go?"

The Keurig spits tea
Into a paper cup.
I wait,
Then say,
"Those tests aren't really about
What you know.
Or if you grow.
I think they're about
Raising doubt."

"What do you mean?" she asks.

I tell her my tale.
She visibly turns pale.

I say, "I fly to Daytona on Sunday morning."
The words seem to hit her without warning.

We talk and chat a little more
Do some writing, which is never a bore.

Then, Tessa tells me
We will have phone conferences
Next week
While I'm in Daytona.

2

Changes

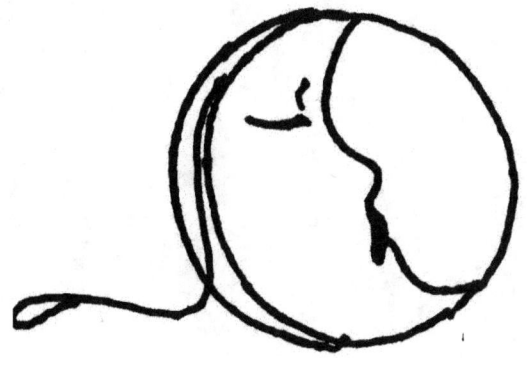

From Bloom's Blue Journal

FLIGHT TO DAYTONA

Not sure what the week holds
For me.

Not sure what I hold
For the week.

My hands are empty,
But my heart is full
Of hidden hope and
An unbidden scope
Of ...

Florida
With all its
Water and sunlight.

Yellow, mellow rays
That warm without and within.

I have school paperwork
For Gran to sign,
Line by line

Each day of the week
As I help her
Perfect and protect her project.

I did not plagiarize.
It would not be wise
And only bring about my demise.

The plane is full.

A fit lady knits
As she sits
Next to me
With yarn on her knee.

Take off is the worst part,
Escaping gravity is an art
Using mechanized power
But just for an hour
Or so today.

"It's a scarf," the lady next to me says.
"For my nephew in New Jersey."

"Nice," I respond,
Though I'm not fond
Of scarves that scratch
Or don't match
What people wear.

I take out my tablet
Open an e-book
This one
Features

A girl who cuts her hair
And dyes it green,
And several people stare
At her look.
Sometimes, she's 'mistook'
For. A. Boy.

And it starts affecting her identity
With increasing severity.

The captain
Tells us we will
Land in
Fifteen minutes
The lady quits
Knitting,
Keeps sitting,
While I keep hitting
A wall inside of me
Where I hope to find something true,
But all I see
Is a blurred reverie
Of what I want the world to be.

I hope Trev is okay,
That he's having a good day,
Hoping for more time to play
With him.

From Bloom's Blue Journal

FLY-RONY

Irony (noun)
A state of affairs or event that seems deliberately contrary to what
one expects and is often amusing as a result.
-Oxford Languages

My dad's a pilot,
And I hate to fly.

Is that irony?
Up High-rony?
Or maybe it's Fly-rony?

At least this flight
Is short.

From Bloom's Blue Journal

THE YO-YO DIARIES PART 1: IN-FLIGHT CONVERSATION WITH MYSELF

At least this flight is short
I'm in a metal tube
30,000 feet above the earth
For what it's worth.

I pull my yo-yo from my backpack,
Never realizing what a fire metaphor it could be
For My Life!

I box breathe.
Inhale four counts.
Hold it for four counts.
Exhale for four counts.

Repeat,
And repeat
What Tessa taught me.

I hear the roar of engines,
The soundtrack of Jurassic World
Through the kid's earphones who sits in front of me.

I smell salted nuts and tired humans
I swim in recirculated air
I'm sweating, but I'm not hot.

I don't have enough room
To do any yo-yo tricks.
Instead, I'll start some journal entries
Dedicated to this toy.

The Yo-Yo Diaries?

At least, it's a short flight.

Inside Daytona International Airport
Sunday, April 7

AIRPORT MEETINGS

I'm aware I'm walking through stories
Of people reunited after being separated
Like a knife's edge, serrated.

Relationships are delicate
A subject and its predicate.
Fragile eggshells?
Clanging bells?

I've experienced both

But then I see Gran,

Smiling, immune to age.
Maybe it's her program,
Age to Page?

I see her wave.
I cave,
Her open arms catch me
I'm bound, but inside,
I'm free.

Tears behind my eyes
Rise, and capsize

Trickle down my face
Feelings, I can't erase.

"Hungry?" she asks.

"Always," I reply
As I dry my eye.
I feel like I can try
To do more than get by.

Her hug is a vacation
From my parents' latest altercation
And the warring nation
Inside of me.

Inside airport Starbucks
SUNDAY, APRIL 7

MOCHA COOKIE CRUMBLES

Gran lets me choose the place,
So, I end today's race
Here.

My punishment?

Sipping a mocha cookie *crumble,*
While my inner walls *tumble,*
And the airport runways *rumble.*

Outside, a bright, sunny, Windexed world
Inside, my stomach unknots from being whirled.

We watch planes soar closer to the stars
Carrying people, faster than cars.

I just want to stop
And talk,
Talk,
Talk,
To Gran.

After a long while,
She excuses herself
And heads toward the restroom.

Inside airport Starbucks
SUNDAY, APRIL 7

COFFEE AND CALLIE

I feel relief after my cry,
Like the tears in
My eyes multiplied
Trying to answer
The Whys?

I pull my journal
From my backpack
And start writing.

Why
    Was I accused?
Why
    Am I here?
Why?
    Is this so hard?

I sigh.

"Sounds serious," a barista says.
She has brown curly hair,
Shorter than Tessa's.
She sits in Gran's place
While Gran is in the restroom.

She wears a nametag,
It says, "Callie."

"Need a refill?" she asks.
I do need a refill
But of what?
Relief,
Chocolate syrup,
Peace,
Whipped cream,
Truth,
And mocha.

"No, thanks," I say.

"What's your name?" she asks.
"Bloom," I reply.

I see Gran leaving the restroom.
She heads back
To the table.

Small talk is not
My strong suit.
What is, I wonder?
Small talk makes me anxious.
What if I say the wrong thing,
Or the other person doesn't really care?

Callie eyes my blue journal.
"You a writer?" she asks.

I nod.

"Then, fight
With your words."

With that, Callie smiles
And leaves the table
Just as Gran returns.

I look for Callie
A few minutes later,
But I don't see her
Anywhere.

Inside airport Starbucks
SUNDAY, APRIL 7

WANNA TALK ABOUT IT?

Gran asks me if I want to talk.
Yes, I actually do.
I picture one of those disembodied jaws,
A chatter chomper?
Just moving its mouth, faster and faster.

But Gran's always been an easy listener,
Kind of like a time-worn rock.
She issues no judgment,
Only quietness and acceptance
While I get to say what I want to say.

Mom would slurp coffee
And personify stress.
Dad would cut me off on every phrase,
His face reflecting the glow
Of his ever-present laptop screen.

"I'll have one of those, too,"
Gran says, nodding at my cup.
"What is it?"

I smile,
And order another mocha cookie crumble for her
At the counter.

Then, I sit across from Gran again.
She smiles at me.

"I got accused of plagiarism . . ."
The words exit me before
I'm aware of the movement
Of my own *chatter chomper*.

"Bloom!" the barista calls.
Gran's drink is ready.
I grab it and a straw
From the counter
And give it to her.

She takes a sip.
"This is good!"

" . . . because I used Odysseus
In my essay," I continue.

Then, I pause.

The steamed milk machine
Burps forth air.

"You'd never do that, Bloom."

More tears deluge my cheeks.
I didn't know Niagara Falls
Waited behind my eyes.

Gran hands me her napkin
And moves to my side of the table.

From Bloom's Blue Journal

THE YO-YO DIARIES PART 2: MY SIDE OF THE TABLE

As a child
I sat alone
On my side of the table,
Unable to shed
The loneliness
That ran through me
With the "only child" label.

I love Mom and Dad,
But when Trev came along
And sat on my side
Of the table,
I felt able.

The other side was reserved for guests.

I hope Trev is okay.

Because now, his sickness sits
In the chair,
Beside me.

It fills the air
And causes so much care.

I can't seem
To bring this yo-yo
Back up to my hand.

At Gran's new condo
Sunday, April 7

THE BOOKS

Gran and I leave Starbucks
And arrive at her new condo,
In Ormond Beach,
Near Daytona.

"You'll love the library.
All of Grandpa's books
In one place,
Finally," she says.

I carry my bags toward my room,
But I stop at the library.

It is open, airy,
With glass walls
Overlooking both the Halifax River
And the Atlantic Ocean.

I look at the shelves and wonder,
How many oceans,
How many rivers
Are in each book
Shelved here?

Books and more books,
Leatherbound,
Hardbound,
Legal,
Nonfiction,
Poetry,
Fiction.

There is even a ladder
With wheels!

In my bedroom at Gran's condo
SUNDAY, APRIL 7

MY NEW ROOM WITH A VIEW

My room at Gran's
Is a symphony of white.
Fluffy pillows,
Shag rugs
A comforter the color of a cloud.

The water below calms me.

The overstuffed chair and lamp
By the glass doors
Beckon me.

"A little reading nook,"
Grandpa would have called it.

Gran pokes her head in
"Settling in okay?"

"This is . . . " I start to say.

She nods, smiles, then says,
"It's what your grandfather wanted,
And he wanted you to have *this* room
Over the library.

He thought the words and thoughts from
So many good books would
Rise, like heat,
To warm your heart and mind."

"When do I start helping you," I ask.

"Tomorrow morning," she says.

"What do I do?"

She sits on the bed,
Pats the comforter.

I sit beside her.

"They're old, they're tired.
They've lived their lives,
But,
They have a lot to say.
'Lived experiences' they call it."

She looks at the ocean,
Then at me, her eyes full of the sea.

"I hoped you could . . . "

I wait for her to finish.

" . . . help them open up,
Get them to express themselves," Gran continues.

I laugh, but I'm not sure why.

Honestly, it's because I picture a room full
Of 80-year-olds writing, with shaky hands,
And hearing aids.

Gran laughs too.

I'm excited.
Helping her sounds fun.

To be fair, the idea of
Writing with them
Intrigues me.

A sigh unexpectedly
Passes through me.

I lean into Gran
And feel her arm
Wrap around my shoulders.

In my bedroom at Gran's condo
SUNDAY, APRIL 7

SUNDAY BEFORE BED

I check my phone.

There's a text from Maya,
And one from Mom.

I read Mom's first.

Trevor's numbers are holding steady.
At least, he's not getting worse.

I then read Maya's.
She's so inquisitive.
"How's it going with your grandma?
So boring here."

She's inviting conversation.
Is this small talk?
Does small talk have to be in-person?
Didn't Tessa say I needed
To engage in more small talk?

I don't answer
Because Maya's conversation
Sounds forced somehow.

I put down my phone.

I'm not one of those teens
Who feels the need
To have a phone glued
To my hand all the time.

I pad downstairs to
Grandpa's library.
Gran left a lamp on.
The light of truth,
Perhaps?

I browse.

It's organized just like a real library.
Fiction, nonfiction, poetry
I stop in myths and legends
I see "The Odyssey"

My heartbeat quickens.

In Grandpa's Library
Sunday, April 7

ODYSSEUS AND ME

Obstacles,
Our connection.

Big ones, small ones,
A Cyclops, A lotus eater,
A plagiarism accusation.

It took Odysseus ten years,
But he made it home to his wife, Penelope.

Will Trevor make it home?

I go back upstairs
Grab a blanket
Nestle into the comfy chair.

I open "The Odyssey."

Then, I see it.

Her name?
Calliope!

Wasn't the barista's name Callie?

I open the book.

I see Ex Libris
On the inside front cover.

William Burwell, Jr.,
My grandfather

I trace his signature
With my finger,
Remembering his hands
Warm, large, protective
With veins along the top
Like tree roots,

Transporting love from
His heart to his
Books, his clients, his family,
And to me.

I felt heavy during
His funeral,
Like I was swimming
Against a strong current,
And I didn't know how long
I could go on.

Is another funeral
In my near future?

I wipe away a tear
And open to the first page
Of "The Odyssey."

3

Calliope

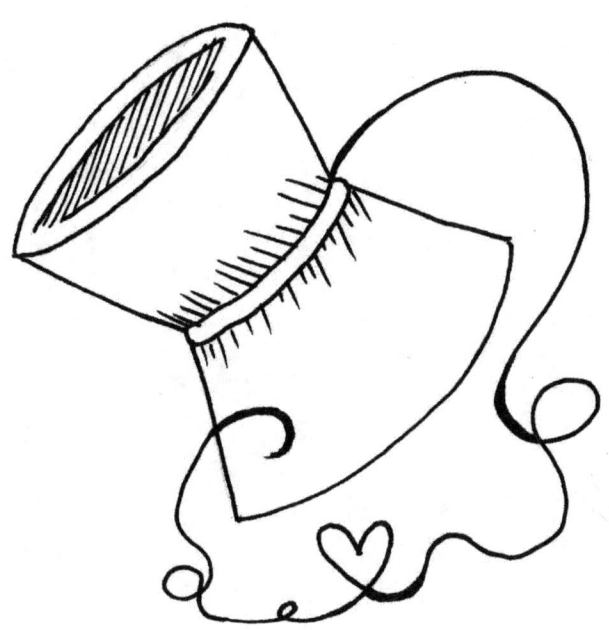

In my bedroom at Gran's condo
Sunday, April 7

CALLIOPE

In Greek mythology,
Calliope was the oldest
Of the nine Greek muses.

Muses were the source
Of all kinds of
Creative inspiration.

She was all about
Epic poetry
And eloquence with words.

Homer dedicated
"The Odyssey" to her.

Why?

Oh, Calliope, Muse of Epic Poetry,
For ideas, you're the source
For words, you're the force.

My question still remains,
Is the barista's name
Short for Calliope?

Is that a coincidence?

In Gran's Kitchen
Monday, April 8

MONDAY MORNING

I walk into the kitchen and see
My grandma wearing red,
A color that makes her look alive.

Her eyes match the blue of the Atlantic
And the deep green of the Halifax.

I smell bacon,
Bacon!
For! Me!
There are eggs and biscuits, too,
But *bacon*? My love language.
It's crispy and crunchy, like a meaty potato chip.

"We'll leave in 15 minutes, Bloom," she says
As she refills her mug with coffee.

"Twenty-seven signed up for today's session.
Should be fun," she says as she takes a sip.

"What do you want me to do again?" I ask,
Reaching for another piece of bacon.

"Just be you,
And follow my lead,
And meet any need

You see," she says taking another sip.
"We want to get them writing,
Cognitive benefits on steroids!"

Gran leaves the kitchen.
After I crunch the last morsel of bacon,
I get curious
And power up my phone.
To search "cognitive benefits of writing."

I know the cognitive benefits of bacon!

In Gran's Kitchen
Monday, April 8

COGNITIVE BENEFITS OF WRITING—PART 1

I click on "Creative Writing and Its Benefits."
I have links in two seconds.

"Creative writing improves brain function
And mental health," it says.
So writing makes us healthier?

I keep reading.
Creative writing helps with "organizing thoughts."
I agree with this one, lots!

I feel I can cope with things
After I write about life's arrows and slings
And other things.

Another benefit is "addressing strong emotions."
Again, I agree since I have oceans
Of feelings swirling in me
At both high and low tides.

The next one is "self-awareness."
Vulnerabilities can escape onto a page
No matter you're age.

"Ready?" Gran is at the door
Purse on her arm.

"In a sec," I say,
And I run upstairs
To brush my teeth
And grab my bag.

I'll read more about the
Cognitive benefits of writing
Later.

Creekside Retirement Home—Meeting Room
Monday, April 8

HELPING OLD PEOPLE

The hallway is full of folded metal walkers
Resting against the wall.
Yellow tennis balls hug their feet.

Inside, each round table is full of senior citizens.
Outside the glass door, seagulls
Fly by.

The birds' whitish gray hue
Matches the hair color of these people.

I don't look forward to small talk,
But I'm here to help.
Yet, I want to yelp
And say, "I didn't plagiarize,
I did not disguise
My words.
It's all a lie!"

Gran walks to the podium in front
"Good morning. Today we start the
Age to Page project.
We have some wonderful
Helpers here."

She introduces a lady named Marta
Then, as if an army arrived from Sparta,
A group of 20 or so high school students walks in.
I can't help but grin.

They sit at different tables.
One of them actually looks like Clark Gable
From "Gone with the Wind."

Gran introduces me as a young writer,
Tells them I'm from Atlanta.

"And this is an English class
From Seabreeze High School.
They're here to participate in
Age to Page as well."
She then asks everyone
To find a journal and a pen or pencil on their tables,
And write a memory or two or three.

I look and see
That some tables
Don't have enough journals.

I grab a stack of them from a box
And walk around delivering them
To writers in need.

I sense someone beside me.
I look,
And I see a young woman.

Brown curly hair peeks out of her gray hoodie.

Callie?

But why would she be *here*?

Creekside Retirement Home—Meeting Room
Monday, April 8

A HAPPY MEMORY OR TWO

I sit at the table in the back,
Surprised by how excited I am
To write.

Gran has asked everyone to write down
A happy memory or two.

"Be sure to include sensory details," she says.
"Tastes, textures, smells, sounds. Make it live.
Oh, and you have ten minutes."

She looks at me.
I nod
And start the timer on my phone.

A tall boy from the Seabreeze group
Sits at my table.
He has clear, mocha-colored skin.
He wears a letterman jacket
With a big "S" on the front.

His hand moves to the center
Of the table
For a journal and a pen.

"Toby," he says.
"Eleventh grade."

"Bloom, ninth," I say.

We both write.

My piece (not surprisingly)
Turns out to be . . .

A poem.

Creekside Retirement Home—Meeting Room
Monday, April 8

ROUGH DRAFT
(Ugh! Forced rhymes yet again, but it's a rough draft)

Trev was four,
And I followed him out the only door.

My plan was to let him play
Outside on that hot July day.

We didn't have a pool
But we celebrated being out of school.

We turned on the water hose,
And we splashed in the water's flow.

We were soaking wet,
But we played until the sun set.

The day tasted like cotton candy,
And we played quite grandly.

Finally, we went in and took showers,
Ate dinner, and then read for hours.

That was a fun summer day!

Creekside Retirement Home—Meeting Room
MONDAY, APRIL 8

ANXIETY, CALLED UP FRONT

After what seems like two minutes
Instead of ten
Fly by,
I hear Gran say,
"Bloom, come on up
And read your piece.
You can show'em
Your poem!"

She laughs at her own rhyme.

Somehow, I find myself ... Bloom (a.k.a. Anxiety in the Flesh)
Moving toward the front of the room.

Callie, or her identical twin, sits in the back,
Writing with some high school kid named Jack.

I hold my journal
Without one kernel

Of confidence.

It is with a belly full of whirling anxiety
I join this society

Of people writing happy memories?

"Hello," I say.
"I'm Bloom, and I wrote
About a hot summer day
I spent with my little brother
A few years ago."

I clear my throat
And hope that what I wrote
Will bob and float
Above my rapid heartbeat.

"My little brother and I
Went outside to play
One hot summer day,

And it actually worked out okay,"
I manage to say.

I look at Gran.
She motions me to go on.

I finally finish
And then say,
"Would one of you like
To share your work?"

Creekside Retirement Home—Meeting Room
MONDAY, APRIL 8

SHARING IS CARING . . . SERIOUSLY?

I don't think
Sharing is caring
in this case.

I think it's
Excruciating
To wait, wondering
if anyone will share.

Do they dare?

Can I go back to Atlanta
Right. Now?

I taste metal in my
Dust-dry mouth.

My palms moisten.

I smell my own sweat,
Sweet from Gran's floral lotion.

"I'll read,"
I hear a deep voice say.

A tall, African-American man
Approaches the podium.

He walks with a slight shuffle,
But his presence cannot be muffled.

Gran waves at me
From the back of the room.
She stands beside Callie.

He begins ...

"My name is Albert Williams.
I have a piece to share."

Creekside Retirement Home—Meeting Room
MONDAY, APRIL 8

ALBERT'S HAPPY MEMORY—FLYING SAUCERS

There's a red brick building
In downtown Jacksonville, Florida.

I went there every Sunday morning
With my grandmother,
My two older sisters,
And a whole lotta cousins
As a boy.

Once I got inside, I'd see rows of flying saucers
In every color of the rainbow,
But they weren't really spacecraft.

Hats, hats, hats!
Those ladies wore a different hat every Sunday.
Grandma wore a green one.

Organ music laughed from the altar
And mixed voices sang as hands clapped.

Then, Reverend got up to preach,
Except I never felt little or small
When I heard the call.

And one day, I responded.
I went down to the front,
And with God, I was blunt.

Felt like a fresh air blew
Through me, revealing what was true.

Finally, we would leave for lunch.
The whole bunch of us,
Going to Aunt Ida's house.

I concentrated on keeping barbecue sauce
Off
my one white dress shirt,
So, I licked the sauce off my fingers,
And I got yelled at
By all my aunties,
But my shirt
Stayed clean!

On those Sundays
Of my childhood.

Creekside Retirement Home—Meeting Room
Monday, April 8

WHO'S NEXT?

Albert's poem is the cause
Of a roomful of applause.

And then I realize
I'm the focus of all their eyes.

But, somehow, Albert's piece
Helps my stress cease.

I see many hands raised,
And I'm no longer dazed.

These poems are a balm
Settling upon me with calm.

I call on Toby this time,
Wondering if he will share a rhyme.

Creekside Retirement Home—Meeting Room
Monday, April 8

TOBY

He stands tall
Behind the podium
Reading a piece about basketball.

How he loves the agility
Each. Player. Possesses.
But also, the fragility of playing ball,
And, of life itself.

He speaks of each player in the game,
And, how he lost a friend he won't name.

"Life is like a game of basketball," he reads.
"We're born, we grow, we rise, then we fall."

"But through the fight,
If we play right,
We win."

In Gran's car
Monday, April 8

ON THE WAY HOME

"How do you think it went?" Gran asks.
I reflect on all my completed tasks.

I remember Albert and Toby, and I smile.
We've already driven two miles.

"Well?" she asks again.

I nod and say,
"I really liked today."

Should I mention Callie, my new friend?
We're already in Gran's garage, so the conversation ends.

In the library at Gran's condo
Monday, April 8

TREV'S CALL

It's 9:07 p.m.
I'm in the chair in Grandpa's library,
Reading.

My phone vibrates.

"Atlanta Children's Hospital" shows on the screen.

"Trev?" I say, dropping the book
To talk to him.

"Bloomie?"
He sounds lonely, small, covered up.

"How are you?!"

"I miss you!" he says.

"I miss you, too.
But it won't be much longer,
I'll be back next week."

"Will you tell me a story?" he asks.

"Of course," I say,
Looking around the room for inspiration.

Then, I remember . . . .

In the library at Gran's house
Monday, April 8

TREV'S STORY

When Trev was about three
I made up stories for him
About two enemy characters
Named Gloom and Glee,

Two warring imaginary foes,
Glee always won in the end.

Glee embodied happy,
But she lived in a world sometimes crappy.
So, she became quite scrappy
Sometimes, she was even yappy.

Of course, she finds ways to defend her joy.

"Once upon a time," I start.
"There was a creature named ..."

Trev yells, "Glee!"

I turn down the volume on my phone.

"Many people tried to steal
Glee's joy," I continue.

"They wanted it because they
Were sad and unhappy,
And they wanted all
Of Glee's cheer."

"One day, Glee found herself
Inside a large hospital.
She could feel sadness dripping from the walls,
And despair rising from the floor like smoke.

"The weight of all that melancholy almost crushed her,
Her joie-de-vivre was hushed there."

"In one room, she heard a boy crying,
Almost like he was dying."

"Glee floated into the room
Where she saw the boy hooked
To tubes and machines."

"She also saw two stuffed animals
On the bed near him.
She quietly scooched them closer
To the boy, and she tucked his covers
Around him."

"Then Glee checked each of the rooms on that floor
And did the same thing for all the patients."

"What about Gloom?" Trev asks.

"Gloom was already there,
But oh, so scared of Glee's love and joy.
So, Gloom left that floor when
Glee arrived."

"Thanks, Bloomie," he says.
I can tell he's fading to black, ready to go to sleep.

Not my best story, I think.
I haven't even gotten to the battle,
But then, I remember Trev and want to sink
Into the delicious covers on my bed here at Gran's.

"Love you, Trev,
I'll see you soon."

"Good night," he says.
"Love you!"

I smile and put away my phone.

Maybe Glee can help me too.

On the way to Creekside Retirement Home
Tuesday, April 9

TUESDAY

"You did great yesterday,"
Gran says as we drive.
We'll be at the facility in five.

"Same thing today?" I ask.

"Yep, but the writing prompt today
Is about life experiences. Yay!"

"Will you share your writing today, Gran?"

Her smile is noncommittal.

"Will that girl in the hoodie
Be there today?" I ask.

"Who?"

"The one who worked
The back table," I answer.

Gran shrugs, then says,
"We're here!"

Creekside Retirement Home—Meeting Room
Tuesday, April 9

LIFE EXPERIENCES

The morning flows like the day before,
Old people are everywhere! So many more.

The Seabreeze students enter
I sit at a table in the center.

Gran begins a couple of minutes before nine
I make sure all have supplies, and I have mine.

"Good morning and welcome to Day Two.
We hope you found writing to be a healthy activity for you."

The participants in the room nod
It feels good, but a little bit odd.

"Bloom? Will you come and share
Our prompt for today ... if you dare?"

Gran says, then laughs.

I walk to the front of the room,
Feeling less anxious, little gloom.

Then, I see Callie wearing red.
She sits by Toby, who has enormous creds

In my book
After yesterday.

"Our prompt today is to write about our life experiences,
Memories, achievements, celebrations, maybe some grievances."

"We'll write for ten minutes," I say.

"Does everyone have a journal and a pen or pencil?"

The Seabreeze students spread out to each table,
Making sure each senior citizen is able
To take part and be stable.
I start the timer on my phone
And go into the zone.

From Bloom's Blue Journal
Tuesday, April 9

EXPERIENCING LIFE

Okay, I'm going to write about why I'm here.

I'm here because I'm fulfilling
A "community service requirement."

Earlier this year, I was accused of plagiarizing
On a state writing test.
I.
Didn't.
Plagiarize,
But that accusation
Pulverized, terrorized, and vaporized my self-respect and confidence.

To be blamed for something like that
Feels like all trust has been broken,
Past, present, and future.

Like a glass tabletop,
Shattered beyond repair.

Maybe the pieces could be glued back together
But the scars will show . . . forever.

I wonder what Mr. Robertson, my English teacher
Thinks of me now.

Will he withdraw
My poem from that national writing contest?

I feel as if I wear a
Scarlet "P"
For everyone to see.

Isn't it funny?
My "P" stands for "Plagiarizer,"
Not "Practical"
In this case.

I hear a distant beeping.
No way! Ten minutes already?

Creekside Retirement Home—Meeting Room
Tuesday, April 9

TURN AND TALK (PART 1)

The war between wanting to write more
And stepping to the podium to start Share Time
Erupts like a volcano in my stomach.

I force myself to stand
And walk to the podium, journal in hand.

"My English teacher back in Atlanta
Sometimes has us turn and talk after we write something,"
I find myself saying to everyone here.

"Basically, that means you find a partner
Somewhere in the room,
You turn or move to that person.
Then you take turns sharing the pieces you just wrote."

I pause. They wait.

"So let's try it."

The room fills with chatter
Like birds chirping before I even finish speaking.

Toby stands and walks toward me,
His journal open.

I guess we're partners.

On Bloom's Cell Phone
Tuesday, April 9

COGNITIVE BENEFITS OF WRITING (PART 2)

I remember more of my research,
As I'm about to share my work with Toby.

Creative writing stimulates the mind.
So true. I feel prickly when I write.

It serves as an emotional outlet.
Yep. When I write about what's bothering me,
I "see" my life with new eyes.

Writing stirs memories.
This is also true,
Especially for these senior citizens.

Creekside Retirement Home—Meeting Room
Tuesday, April 9

TOBY'S PIECE: BEAUTIFUL BUBBLES

I was at the beach last summer,
School had just let out.

My friends and me, yeah,
Were meeting some girls there.

I had never seen a jellyfish before,
Being from Tennessee, originally.

Anyway, I saw these colorful pouches
On the sand,
Like shiny bubbles.
I was so intrigued.

I thought they had come out of dolphins
Or maybe whales.

Anyway, they're beautiful
When you look at them,
Really examine them.

I guess everything touches on

The Beauty
That's already there
If you just open your eyes,
And see.

Creekside Retirement Home—Meeting Room
Tuesday, April 9

TURN AND TALK (PART 2)

"Okay," I say.
"Find another partner
And share your pieces."

But I don't have to say it
Because the room sounds like
The school cafeteria
During second lunch,
Or one of those professional sound effects
Called "a crowd" or "indistinct chatter."

The old people are lit!
So are the young people.

Callie walks toward me.
I hope she's going to share her piece
With me.

Instead, she says,
"Good job, Bloom.
Keep it going.
Writing heals."

And then she's gone,
But I see a piece of paper? A note?
On the podium.

"Bloom" is written across the front
In an old-style script. Calligraphy, is it?

Makes sense.
Callie using calli-graphy!

My heartbeat quickens.

In Gran's car on the way to her condo
Tuesday, April 9

DRIVING HOME ON TUESDAY

Gran bursts with energy
Talking about the synergy
Experienced today.

She smiles and beams,
Was it real or a dream?
All the words everyone wrote.

"It's working, I think,"
She says, then takes a drink
From her tumbler of tea.

I can't wait to talk to Trevor,
Maya, Mom, Dad, Whoever!
I look at Gran and laugh.

From Bloom's Blue Journal
Tuesday, April 9

THE YO-YO DIARIES PART 3: WRITING TRUES

Expressing myself through writing
Is like letting ice melt on your tongue
On a 110-degree day.

It cools,
It soothes,
It quenches,
A thirst I don't realize I have.

Writing is a compass,
Pointing my thoughts,
Fears, anxieties

North
To a Truth
I know is there

Somewhere.

If I keep writing,
Will I find it?
Will I be able
To stop this bouncing yo-yo
Called my life?

In my room at Gran's condo
Tuesday, April 9

CALLIE'S NOTE

I hold Callie's note in my hand,
The one she left on the stand.

My hands tremble as I open it and read.
"You're a listener, Bloom,
Listeners are rare in any room.
They are often isolated,
Their skills not at all elevated
In your world.

"Listeners hear the Muse,
Then they choose
To create
Instead of imitate.

"Meet me at the bookstore
Tomorrow afternoon. I'll tell you more."

I pause and think about what it takes to listen,
To prioritize the job of ears.

I pull out my phone,
And search for traits of a good listener.

Wow!
Here goes.

Good listeners . . .
Are fully present
React in the moment
Don't listen to respond
Don't have an agenda
Don't jump in to give advice
Never interrupt
Are patient
Show interest in what the speaker is interested in
Summarize what they have heard

Callie gave me quite the compliment.
Is it true in my life at this moment?

Creekside Retirement Home—
Meeting Room before the session begins
WEDNESDAY, APRIL 10

WEDNESDAY'S PROMPT

Today's writing topic? Imagination.
Something my school seems to ration!

I fixed Gran's breakfast, had her coffee ready,
Can't explain why I'm so heady.

Looking around, I see we are ready to begin
These old folks are truly *all in*!

I ask Toby to head to the front with me,
He unfolds his long frame and walks slowly.

I hand him the prompt to read,
Thankfully, he takes the lead.

"Yo, good morning," he says and then smiles,
"We're going to write about the imagination with style."

"Write about using your creativity
Or an enjoyable imaginative activity.

He pauses, then continues ...

"We all have ten minutes
Let's write without limits."

He sets his phone's timer and sits
To write. No one quits.

From Bloom's Blue Journal
WEDNESDAY, APRIL 10

"WHAT DO YOU IMAGINE NOW?"

Times I've used my imagination?

I remember going to Gran and Grandpa's
Old house
As a little girl.

It smelled like salt,
And cedar,
A natural, clean outdoor fragrance.

Grandpa was a successful attorney,
And he was so imaginative.

Sometimes, he would read to me.
We snuggled into his big armchair.
I don't know where he got all those picture books,
From Gran, I guess.

He would read the book to me,
But before he would turn a page, he'd ask,
"What do you imagine now?"

I got so excited,
I couldn't speak fast enough
To express my thoughts and ideas.

One time, Gran brought
A fresh stack of books home
From the library where she worked.

One of them was called,
"Coco the Carrot" by Steven Salerno.

It's about a carrot
Who leaves her vegetable bin in the fridge
To sail to France on a large ship
And become a famous hat designer
(Grandpa taught me that the fancy word
For hatmaker is milliner).

Oh, how I loved that book
And imagining my six-year-old self
Making hats like Coco the Carrot.
I can still see the artwork,
Of Coco, her best friend Antoine (a monkey)
And the famous Parisian designer
Coco works for.

"And time!" Toby says
Breaking into my memories
And my writing rhythm.

My conclusion?

Time and Imagination
Are mortal enemies!

Creekside Retirement Home—Meeting Room
Wednesday, April 10

WEDNESDAY'S SHARE TIME
(A.K.A. "Amusement Parks for Ants")

Toby just goes right there,
He motions to a lady who gets out of her chair.

She walks up front with her journal and pen,
Her profile reminds me of a Carolina wren.

She says, "Mildred is my name,
I hope this piece isn't . . . lame."

She cuts her eyes toward me and shoots a smile,
Will her piece require listening for a while?

"When I was little,
I had a playmate named Patrick.
We were neighbors.
We lived in North Carolina back then,
And Patrick and I played outside
After school nearly every day.
Patrick amazed me.
He ate rope,
Caught frogs,
And started fires with a magnifying glass.
One day, we gathered sticks,
Acorns, and rocks."

"What should we make?" he asked.

"I thought for a minute."

"An amusement park for ants," I said.

"And crickets, and grasshoppers,
And maybe some lizards," Patrick added.

"We got to work
Creating slides, a swing set,
And a merry-go-round,
Out of sticks, rocks, and mud!
It was so much fun."

Mildred pauses and looks up
From her journal.

Applause blooms
In the room.

In Gran's Car
WEDNESDAY, APRIL 10

WEDNESDAY'S TRIP HOME

"Can we go by the mall
On the way home, Gran?"

"Sure," she says.
"Need anything specific?"

"Nope. Just wanna look around the bookstore,
Check out their poetry section."

"Okay, I'll drop you off
And run into Bath and Body Works."

No. Surprise. There.
My grandmother is the Soap Queen of Daytona Beach
Probably of Florida!

"Perfect," I reply.

Suddenly, I'm tired.
I yawn.

Tessa says sudden sleepiness
Can be a sign of anxiety.

"You okay?" Gran asks.

I nod.

"I'll get a hot chocolate
In the café."

At the Books-A-Million in Volusia Mall
WEDNESDAY, APRIL 10

BOOKS-A-MILLION ON A WEDNESDAY EVENING

Relief washes over me
As soon as I enter the bookstore.

Its brown carpet, beige walls,
And seemingly endless shelves of books
Bring me peace

And energy.

My fatigue is gone.

I browse a table of Young Adult books
Near the front of the store.

I temporarily forget
I'm there to meet Callie.

I look up and notice a series
Of large, framed black-and-white
Photographs of people,
Reading,
Using their minds
And imaginations.

One photo depicts an Asian man
In an armchair *reading* a book.

Another photo shows a girl,
About seven years old,
Reading a book to her baby brother.

I remember Trev.

Another photo shows a teenage girl
Sitting on a park bench under the sun
Reading.

Then, I find the Poetry Shelf.
Five rows,
Full of poetry books.

Dickinson, Frost, Neruda,
Poets we have read in Mr. Robertson's
English class back home.

And then I see
A poetry collection
By Billy Collins.

I love Billy Collins!

I pick up
"Musical Tables,"
And chuckle at the
Painting of the cow
Lying on a couch
On the front cover.

Maybe it's a 'cowch'?
I chuckle at my own pun.

I see something red in my peripheral vision.
I look up and see Callie.

"So glad you came.
Want a coffee?" she asks.

The memory of why I'm here
Hits me like the rush of hot air when you open a hot oven.

"Hi! Yes! But hot chocolate, please,
Not coffee."

We head to the café.
I remember I'm holding the Billy Collins book.
She steps behind the counter,
And a moment later, she says,
"Here . . . ."
She hands me a cup of hot chocolate with no lid

But. With. Mountains. Of. Whipped. Cream. On. Top.

How. Did. She. Know?

We sit
Opposite each other
At a round wooden café table.
"Thanks for coming," she says.

I attempt a sip
But my drink is too hot.
The liquid burns my lip.
Reminds me of earlier
When the timer went off
And I had to stop writing.

My Imagination Was Scalded!

"Remember how I told you you're a listener?"

I nod.

"You're also a poet,
You have a gift."

I blush, look down,
Uncomfortable.

"Your grandfather had the gift too."

I look at her.
Do they have records of poets
Up on the mountaintop
Where the Muses live?

"I met him years ago
When he read 'The Odyssey.'"
She pauses, remembering.

"Look in that book, Bloom,
You'll learn so much more."

She looks back to the café counter.
Three people are in line.

"I've gotta go," she says.
"Keep up the good work."

Callie leaves the table
As Gran enters the café,
Carrying two big bags
Full of soaps and lotions,
I'm sure.
"Whatcha got there?" she asks,
Looking at my book.

"What?"
I slowly return to Billy
And my hot chocolate.

"You okay, dear?"

Gran looks at her watch.
"Goodness, it's late.
I need to get you home and feed you."

I look back at the café counter,
But a young man wearing
A black baseball cap
Is working behind the counter.

Callie is nowhere
To be seen.

Grandpa's library in the condo
WEDNESDAY, APRIL 10

LATE WEDNESDAY NIGHT

I find myself in Grandpa's library,
My first choice always, with no bribery.

For some reason, my anxieties cease.
When I breathe in these books, I feel peace.

Callie's words revisit me,
I head to a shelf, bend my knee.

I find myself facing many spines,
Grandpa wanted these books to be mine.

I pull out his copy of The Odyssey
A strange calmness envelops me.

I recline on the chaise and begin to read,
I have a sense I may find something I need.

In the margins, I see his copious notes,
Grandpa's comments on descriptions and quotes.

Then I see it, a small drawing of her.
But it can't be Callie, of that, I am sure.

I must be really tired, my eyes playing tricks,
I am intrigued, but I shut the book. Quick.

This is weird, this whole situation,
I'm going to bed, to get some relaxation.

In Gran's car on the way to Creekside Retirement Home
Thursday, April 11

THURSDAY MORNING

I woke up too late to eat breakfast,
But I drank some orange juice.

My eyelids are a garage door,
When the power goes out,
Stuck in the down position.

Gran is chipper.
She didn't even have
Coffee this morning!

Did she really raise my mom?

"... All about our fears," she says.

"What?" I say, realizing I haven't been listening.

Sorry, Callie!
Listeners aren't always listening.

"The prompt for today. Our fears," she replies.

My stomach clinches.

I hope Toby runs the show today.

Creekside Retirement Home—Meeting Room
Thursday, April 11

THURSDAY'S SESSION

It's two minutes before nine.
Gran stands in the back,
Talking and laughing.

Where's Toby?

I'm floating in humid air
Of La Florida, the flower.

Gran's still chatting.

I approach the podium.

The room quiets.

Toby walks in.
I exhale.
I look for Callie,
Don't see her anywhere.

"Good morning," I say.

"Today, we're writing about our fears.
Fears from childhood or first jobs,
Nightmares or scary people
Or something scaring you right now."

I pause, then say, "We will write for ten minutes."

"I want 20 or 30!" Mildred yells from her seat.

A mild uproar of agreement fills the room.

I look at Gran,
She nods.

"Okay, we will write for 15 minutes," I say.

I start the timer on my phone
And once more enter the zone.

From Bloom's Blue Journal

MY FEARS: A BRIEF HISTORY

I used to imagine a witch under my bed,
Cackling at the thought of finding me dead.

Probably a normal childhood fear
But it definitely stole my cheer.

Another time, a big brown roach crawled on me
Whirled its antennae and perched on my knee.

But lately, it's Trev who has me so scared
Will he live? Didn't realize how much I cared.

And there's also Mom and Dad's marriage
All that fighting. Can it be salvaged?

And now, a plagiarism accusation
What effect will it have on my education?

I guess my worry is a choice,
That can shut down my voice.

I try to focus on good things instead.
Inside, what slowly goes away is my dread.

Creekside Retirement Home—Meeting Room
Thursday, April 11

WRITING WRAIN?

I finish before the timer buzzes.

I look around.

The room is busy, but quiet.

I feel as though I'm in the eye
Of a creativity hurricane.

The wind of ideas,
A lightning flash to jot them down
Before they disappear,

And the rain ...
The soothing, cleansing rain of writing.

Washing thoughts from your head
Onto the paper

And then, the relief

Of

Writing Wrain!

Creekside Retirement Home—Meeting Room
Thursday, April 11

SHARE TIME: HAROLD

"My name is Harold Murray.
I'm 82 years old.
I was married to Lucille for 52 years.
She passed away last year.
We have one son, a doctor,
Who lives in Colorado."

"Here's what I wrote."

Harold clears his throat,
Opens his journal.

"I first went to Viet Nam
As a nineteen-year-old boy.
I fought with ground troops
Near Hanoi."

"I didn't know what fear was
Until I had to hide in camo,
Not knowing if the ground
Would blow up in my face,
Or a gun barrel would poke my back."

"I had panic attacks,
There on the ground."

"The only thing,
The only thing,
The only thing
That helped
Were the verses
My Grandma taught me."

"One of them goes something like,
Don't anxious about anything,
But in every situation, pray with thanksgiving,
And let God know what you want."

"Then it says,
You'll get peace
In your heart and mind.
Those verses got me through Nam,
But also through life when I got back
And saw a changed culture."

"I'm not saying I don't have any fears anymore,
But I know the truth,
And I have peace,
An incomprehensible solace,
And I hope you do too."

From Bloom's Blue Journal

THE YO-YO DIARIES PART 4: WHOSE TRUTH?

I always thought
Truth
Was an
Unmovable
Force,

Not a yo-yo,
Going up, down, and all around,
Based on our subjective
Opinions
or
Emotions.

Like when you're little
And you learn the school lessons
About
Fact
Vs.
Opinion

Or, when you tell a lie,
You know
In Your Heart
It's false and wrong.

But where did I get that
Idea?

Honestly, it probably came from Grandpa
Our "talks" about books and thoughts.

He legit taught me
Logic
And
Rhetoric
When he read to me,
But I didn't know it then.

And now, Harold gets up
And reads about his *fear*
Diving into his soft flesh
Like a *spear*!

My worries and anxieties pale
What he went through was a nail
P
i
e
r
c
i
n
g
His heart
And mine.

I remember stories,
About someone else with piercings
And furious, fierce flings

Of a cat of nine tails
Leaving bloody trails
Of flesh in its wake.
Is that story real or a fake?

What's truly true?
Whose is the correct view?

They say I plagiarized,
But I only summarized
What Grandpa taught me
When we read "The Odyssey."

Creekside Retirement Home—Meeting Room
Thursday, April 11

TOBY TAPS ME ON THE SHOULDER AND . . .

. . . Bounces me from my
Writing reverie,
With his signature
Jokes and brevity.

"You leading or reading?" he asks.

I don't know how much time has passed,
Since Harold read, and thoughts of truth surpassed . . .

My temporary anxieties.

"You going to share?
Do you dare?" Toby inquires again.

I shake my head,
Still navigating the world
My writing took me to.

He says, "Guess it's my turn."

I reply, "Make it burn."

Creekside Retirement Home—Main Library
Thursday, April 11

IDENTITY
(by Toby)

I'm Black,
African American,
Although African Americans
Can be White.

Is that right?

People tell me
I talk like a White guy
"That's good," they say.
"It will help you get by."

Is that true?
Doesn't it matter who

You
    Really
        Are?

That's what scares me,
Growing up in this murky sea
Of
Forced
Identities.

Creekside Retirement Home—Meeting Room
Thursday, April 11

GRAN TAKES OVER

There's a rumble in the room
As if we're on a plane about to zoom
Through the sky.
At first, I wonder why
Then, I realize we've reached so high
With these older people writing
Some of them fighting
With the words that come through
All that insulation and all that glue
That makes every one of us sticky
As we keep to ourselves, staying prickly
Until someone or some thing
Breaks us apart, lets us sing
Our words,
Flying like birds
Upward!

Gran's voice interrupts
It's all rather abrupt.
But what she says
Lifts me from my creative daze.

"Good morning. As you finish,
We have an opportunity to publish
All your writing efforts
Into lovely, professional booklets."

There are "oohs" and "aahs,"
Even some "rahs,"
As these people realize
Their words are going to be memorialized.

"Tomorrow, we will do one more writing exercise,
That way, you'll have plenty
Of entries to choose from," she says.

The room fills with chatter,
As they share pieces that matter.

I must readily confess
Gran's program is a roaring success.

Creekside Retirement Home—Meeting Room
Thursday, April 11

MOM'S CALL

I hear an insistent buzz,
Forgot about my phone in my writing fuzz.

Mom's calling. I'm sure she has news.
Reality's here. Must leave my creative muse.

I walk into the hall,
Wanting and not wanting to stall
This call.

"Hi, Mom!"

"How's it going, honey?"

"Great, actually.
I love it here,"

"How's Trev?" I ask
Before I mean to.

"More tests," she says with a sigh.
"Still waiting for the official diagnosis.
But," she continues,
"I'm calling to remind you
Your flight leaves tomorrow night
Around seven," she pauses.

"I'll call Gran and remind her too. We have missed you!"

Creekside Retirement Home: Meeting Room
THURSDAY, APRIL 11

TOBY'S INVITATION

I walk back into the meeting room.
Toby's standing there,
Holding a piece of paper and a broom?
He hands me the paper,
And I read it.

It's a small, colorful flyer,
Inviting me
To a party at the beach
With his youth group, a local teen nation.
I'm honored that he reached
Out to me.

Life moves faster here
So much living in just one week,
But my head is so clear
Don't feel like I'm such a freak
Anymore.

I smile and nod my head,
As Toby sweeps away the day's paper shreds.

Creekside Retirement Home: Meeting Room
Thursday, April 11

CALLIE'S CONVERSATION

As I prepare to leave the facility that afternoon
I see a flash of red and hear a lilting tune.

Is it Callie? I hope so.
So much to tell her before I go.

Gran's busy packing up her stuff.
We have time. Hopefully, it's enough.

"I fly home tomorrow," I say to start our talk.
"Let's go outside," she says as we walk.

"I'm not real; I live in your imagination,
But please keep up your investigation,
And find The Truth
While you're in your youth."

"You'll find me in numerous pages,
Of good books from all cultures, all ages.
But if you're seeking Truth that sets you free
Try The Book. It will help you see."

Her words hit hard as moisture forms in my eyes,
Suddenly, I don't look forward to tomorrow's goodbyes.

4

Clearing

At Daytona Beach
Thursday, April 11

SALT WATER

Gran drops me off at the beach.
I look for Toby in the group
The sky is stormy, a cloudy soup.

Kids laugh, play volleyball.
Toby taps me on the shoulder.
Feels like I've been hit by a boulder.

He introduces me to a man named Kurt, a pastor,
And lots of other kids our age.
They seem joyful, let out of their cage.

In a few minutes,
We eat hamburgers and hot dogs.
I then notice an incoming fog.

The cloudiness adds mystery
As Pastor Kurt starts,
Walking in the shallows to a kid with a side part.

Pastor Kurt shares a few words of his own.
"A lot of kids today,
Are searching. Many of them stray."

"But there's only one way.
I know many of you are unsure
But the words I share are pure."

"You're looking for something real.
It's Truth you're searching for
And, it will change you at your core."

By now, Pastor Kurt
Is waist-deep in the water
Tears in my eyes, don't know what's the matter.

He dunks Side-part Kid in the water.
Later, Pastor Kurt says hi to me.
I feel something has been set free.

"I've never read that book," I say.
"It's not bad," he says. "Some parts are really keen,
"Try the book of John, it goes scene by scene."

Pastor Kurt moves on
Talks to other young people,
He's cool, treats them all equal.

Callie told me Truth is universal
It's always been here.
I look to the ocean,
And the murky water is now clear.

Has the fog lifted too?

That dunking under water was symbolic
Of death and then life,
Are they two sides of one knife?

I think of Trev
His life, a bright flare.
I then mouth a silent prayer.

But, I'm not the God-fearing type.
My dad says religion is just another myth
That Zeus, Artemis, and Apollo go with . . . .

Yet, something changed here this evening,
I feel acceptance
And some sort of transcendence.

In Gran's car

Thursday, April 11

PART OF MYSELF

Gran picks me up around nine
"How was it?" she asks.
I say, "It was fine."
But, to be honest, I'm wearing no mask.

We get home, and I find
I'm really quite tired.
I take a shower to unwind,
And yet, inside me there's a fire.

I pad into Grandpa's library
Kneel down at my shelf.
There's a book there inscribed to me
I feel I'm finding part of myself.

I open it and can't believe my eyes.
I see Grandpa's notes and a sketch of her.
I realize again this culture is full of lies,
Of what this book says, can I be sure?

Then on the next page, I see,
"The Truth shall set you free."

At Gran's condo
Thursday, April 11

MAYA'S CALL

My phone vibrates on the floor
Beside me
Throwing me from my reverie.

It's Maya, back in Atlanta
Probably still involved in lots of drama.

I pick up.

"Hey," I say.

"Hey! Have you heard?"

My heart rides a roller coaster down a big hill.

"Heard what?" I respond.

"Your writing!"

I pause. Does she mean the test essay,
Or the poem in that contest?

"Which piece?" I ask.

"The one Mr. Robertson said you should submit.
The poem about searching for what's true or something?"

"Yeah."

"It won," she says.
"Don't know about mine yet."

"Wait, what?"

"Yeah, your poem won some national award.
Dr. Dey read it on the announcements this morning."

"No way," I say.

"Way," Maya replies.
"Anyhoo, you coming back to school
Next week?"
Suddenly, it seems as though
I've been away at least a year.

"Oh, yeah," I say.
"I fly back tomorrow night."

"Well, congrats!
Didn't know if you knew."

"No . . . , I didn't.
Thanks for calling, Maya," I say.

"Yep," she says.
"See you Monday!"

"See ya."

At Gran's condo
Friday, April 12

FRIDAY MORNING

It's stereotypical to love Fridays, and I do,
But today is different, as I feel somewhat blue.

And, I'm surprised at what I now find to be true.
I seem to be attached to these elderly people with glue.

Who knew
What writing could do?

Creekside Retirement Home—Meeting Room
Friday, April 12

WHERE'S TOBY?

I want to talk to him,
Tell him about Maya's call,
But also ask him about that beach

Thing

Because my heart has been released from a

Sling

And I want to

Fling

Off my old ways and

Sing!

Creekside Retirement Home: Meeting Room
Friday, April 12

FRIDAY'S PROMPT

Gran asks me to lead.
It's actually not that hard anymore.

"Good morning,
Today is our last day
Of the Age to Page Program."

I notice several residents
Already writing,
Not fighting
The flow of words.

The door opens,
Toby enters carrying a gift bag
With pink and red tissue paper popping out
Like an impressionistic painting of a bouquet of roses.

"Our prompt today," I continue,
"Focuses on the future.
Your hopes, your dreams,
What you hope to accomplish
While you're here on earth."

I pause for just a moment
Let everyone's ideas foment
The oncoming evolution
Of a thought revolution.

"We will begin . . . now."

I set the timer on my phone
And start writing.

From Bloom's Blue Journal

THE YO-YO DIARIES PART 5: HOPES AND DREAMS

For me, they're simple,
I guess.

I want to speak the truth.
I want to seek the truth.
I want to find the right truth
And
Write
Truth.

I want to be filled with Truth.
I want to listen to Truth.

And.
Be.
Changed.
By.
The.
Truth.

Some people (like my dad) might think that's uncouth.

Now I know,
Truth is more like a sword,
Constant and sure,
Not a yo-yo,
Moving up, down, and all around.

I'd also like to submit more
Of my writing in contests.

I guess I'd also like to find a
Youth group like Toby's
Back home in Atlanta,

And use my voice,
Say something worthy amidst all the noise.

At Creekside Retirement Home—Meeting Room
Friday, April 12

TRUTH DOESN'T WAIT

My phone vibrates
Before I finish my entry.

It's Mom, texting me,
"Available?"

Sounds serious.

I excuse myself,

Walk into the hall
I make the call.

"Mom?"

"It's Trev, honey."
Her voice is hoarse, cracked.

"What is it?"

"Well ..."

"The truth, Mom ...."

"The tests have come back.
Trev will start chemotherapy
And he might need a bone marrow transplant," she pauses.

"The doctors say
Chemo's the only way."

Tears splash on the cover of my journal.
I picture my little brother, just a kernel
With so much growing up to do.

"Anyway, he's asking for you,
And I thought you might come by
The hospital in the morning."

"Of course, Mom," I say.

"Oh, thank you, honey,"
I hear her inhale, then exhale.
"I know it's a lot to take in," she says.
"I've got to go now,
The doctor's here,
But your father will meet your flight
At the airport tonight."

There's another pause.

"I love you, Bloom."

"Love you, too."

She ends the call,
I'm still in the hall.

I slump into a chair
And cry.
Why Trev?
Why leukemia?

A white Kleenex appears
In front of me.

I grab it,
Blow my nose.
I notice a pair of Nike Air Force Ones
Parked beside me.

Then, I'm aware
Of someone sitting next to me
It's Toby.

He offers me another Kleenex
And puts his arm around me.

The tears keep falling.

The gift bag appears in front of my face.
I'm surprised, then see something with lace
On the cover.

"It's for you . . . from all the Seabreeze kids," he says.

I reach into the bag
And feel a book with a tag.

It's a new journal with a lace cover
Feel like I'm seeing a long, lost lover
So, I hug it.

"There's a pack of pens in there too," Toby says.

"Thank you. This may be the nicest gift I've ever gotten," I say.

I put the journal back into the bag
And know when I use it, my words won't lag.

"There's something else in there," he says.

And I soon know
They've given me a new …

Yellow
Yo-yo!

Phone call with Tessa, the therapist
FRIDAY, APRIL 12

ANOTHER PHONE CALL!

My phone buzzes again
With a call from
Family Counseling Services
Back home in Atlanta.

For a moment,
I'm tempted
To let it go to
Voice mail.

But I don't.

"Hello?" I say.

"Hi, Bloom! How's it going?"
Tessa's voice sounds relaxed,
Hydrated.

"I'm good.
I'm really good," I say.

"Yeah?
How's your grandmother's
Program going?"

"Oh, my gosh!
I love it!
It's been so fun
Writing with these people!"
I'm surprised I open up
To Tessa so easily.

Is this
Small talk?

"So, you've been writing too?" she asks.

"Yep, and I've made friends!"

"Okay, well, you sound great.
I'm going to make a note
About our chat,
And I'll see you soon,
When you get back to Atlanta,"
She says.

"I've almost
Used every page
In my journal,"
I tell her.

"Oh, yeah?" she replies.
"We'll get you a new one
When you come in again,
Okay?"

"Sounds good."

"Alright then,
Bye, Bloom.
Glad you're doing so well."

"Bye, Tessa."

I hit the End button
And realize I'm smiling.

At Daytona International
AIRPORT, FRIDAY, APRIL 12

PRE-FLIGHT

Toby rode with Gran and me
To the airport.

Before we got here,
We stopped at Starbucks,
Gran's treat (always).

I got another mocha cookie crumble
(So did Gran).
Toby ordered a strawberry lemonade.

Now, my heart is wind worn, exposed.
Eroded by air and water,
And yet, being in this moment
With these two people,
I feel secure.

They drop me off
In the Departing Flights Lane
A skycap takes my bag.

Gran hugs me first,
"Love you, Bloomie!
I'll fly up next week
And check on Trev."
She gets back into her car.

Then Toby
Gives me a hug,
He feels like my favorite
Crocheted blanket
Keeping me warm and safe.

I don't trust my voice.

"Praying for you," he says.

"I'll text you," I say in a whisper.

He nods and waves.

On the airplane
Friday, April 12

THOUGHTS ON MY FLIGHT HOME

Leaving Florida and new friends behind.
Entering Georgia with my vision more defined.

Departing from my blinded state.
Arriving home with a fresh fate.

I know now I've been seeking Truth.
Perhaps I've found it in my youth.

I examine my new yo-yo
It casts a yellowish glow
On my journal blue
I'm starting to like this golden hue.

5

Chances

At the Atlanta airport
Friday, April 12

MY DAD

I see him
Before he sees me.
He's standing, watching
At the end
Of the sky bridge.
Hands in his pockets,
Like usual.

When I was little,
I thought my dad was Superman,
the Incredible Hulk,
and Spiderman
All in one
Tall Jamaican man.

I stood with my hands in my pockets
To be like him.
He could do no wrong
In my eyes.
But childlike eyes become more focused
As the years go by.

I realized my dad is human
With a serious anger problem,
Quick-tempered,
Coming *unglued*
At anything,
As he flies around the world.
Maybe he's searching for Truth

Too.

I think I was about 12
When I realized
What the phrase,
"Walking on eggshells" meant.

He sees me and waves.
I give him a hug.
"Good to see you," he says.

I hope no shells crack today.

Bloom's house
Friday, April 12

ARRIVING HOME

I do not know
If home has changed
Or if I have,
But everything *looks* different.

I see with new eyes.

Trevor is looking forward to seeing me
Tomorrow morning.

I will tell him a new story about Glee and Gloom
And read to him in his hospital room.

I might ask if I can spend the night
Give Mom a break
And give me a chance to write

In. My. New. Journal.

Then Monday, it's back to school
Learn the outcome of "breaking"
the plagiarism rule.
I wonder what
The investigators found.

Guess I have my own obstacles,
Guess we all do,
Just like Callie said,
Just like Odysseus did.

Mom is at the hospital with Trev.

As I lie on my bed
Processing this past week
I realize how much I've missed her.

Bloom's house
Friday, April 12

CHEMO CONVERSATION

A call came in a little while ago,
Dad paused the crime show
We were watching.

I could tell he had news
I saw his tears; I read his cues,
He started talking
In fits and spurts.

"They start chemo on Trev soon,"
Dad says, then exhales loudly.
"He's going to ...
Need all of us to be strong."

I'd rather write my response in my journal,
But now I know
It's okay to speak up.
It's good to share my thoughts,
And my voice,
So, I try it.

"I researched chemotherapy on the flight home," I say.
"Success rates are high."

Dad almost trips over the coffee table,
As he moves to sit beside me.

He puts his arm around me,
Draws me close.

I move into the hug,
Knowing we both need comfort,
And remembering how things used to be
Between us.

"I'm sorry, Bloom,
I haven't been here much."

I'm not sure if he means
Physically,
Emotionally,
Or some other way?
I decide to take the risk . . . .
"I love you, Dad,
And I know you
Love us."

He sniffles
And rubs his face.

"For so long, though,
I felt like I couldn't speak up
And say what I really wanted to say.
Like I'd be punished if I did,
So I just stopped."

I take a deep breath.

"I realize now
That just made it all worse."

I can tell he's listening to me.

"But, this week,
In Florida,
I feel like I found something

Real,

Something I have been looking for."

"So," I say after a pause.
"I want you to know
I'll be strong.
I'm in this for the long
Haul."

Dad's tears don't stop,

And somehow, I know
The last eggshells have cracked.
There will be no more broken pieces
Scratching my bare feet.

At Atlanta Children's Hospital
Saturday, April 13

SATURDAY MORNING

I see Jeffy the Giraffe's spotted head,
Poking out from the covers
Before I see Trev, sleeping.

He's hooked to more machines
Than the last time I was here.

I approach his bed
And lightly touch
His arm
Wrapped around Jeffy.

Mom is suddenly beside me
I didn't even see her.
I lean into her open arms
And the tears fall.

She's battled obstacles, too.

I see that now.

At Atlanta Children's Hospital
SATURDAY, APRIL 13

IN TREV'S ROOM

Trev stretches and then wakes up fast
He's thinner than when I saw him last.

He sees me and gives me a silly, big grin,
This moment is a win-win.

"Bloomie!" he yells, wiggling all over,
"Trev!" I shout back and straighten his covers.

His stretches his arms toward me
I'm even more full of empathy.

I climb into bed beside him,
Gratefulness filling me to the brim.

"I'm going to the café," Mom says. "Be back soon."
"Do you want anything? It's nearly noon."

I shake my head and look on Trev's tray.
I grab a cookie and tell her I'm okay.

I pick up Jeffy and make him dance
Trev laughs; He's got a fighting chance.

I feel empowered, ready to share
Facts with him and show him I care.

But I know he wants a story first
So, I dig deep and let the creativity burst.

In Trev's Room at Atlanta Children's Hospital
SATURDAY, APRIL 13

MOM RETURNS

When Mom returns to the room
I'm deep in a story featuring Glee and Gloom.

She laughs when she sees me, a lovely sound.
But she knows nothing about what I've found.

I finish the story with a cute little pose
She smiles, but there's something she knows.

"I need to talk to you about the charge at the school,
Dr. Dey and I have spoken about the plagiarism rule."

I nod and ask if she'd like to go home for the night,
I tell her I'll stay with Trev, she can rest from this fight.

A grateful look covers her face,
I know she's been running at a rapid pace.

"It's okay, Mom. I brought a change of clothes."
Her expression relaxes, releases its woes.

In Trev's room at Atlanta Children's Hospital
Saturday, April 13

SIDE EFFECTS

In the afternoon, a nurse comes in
She checks on Trev, offers me her grin.

"You're the big sister I've heard so much about.
He's your Number One fan without a doubt."

"Can we talk about side effects? What to expect?" I ask.

"Depends on the kid, but I'll be quick and direct," she says.

"He will probably get nauseous and lose his hair.
There's a drug for the nausea, about the other? He may not care."

"He'll also feel weaker and need to carry a lighter load,
But after six weeks, he can walk his old road."

"Trev will come twice a week after treatment starts,
About an hour each time. We'll keep track on his charts."

I thank her for all the information,
And pray that Trev's cells have a transformation.

In Trev's Room at Atlanta Children's Hospital
SATURDAY, APRIL 13

PUZZLES

The hospital chaplain brought Trev puzzles and toys
Things he thought would amuse little boys.

I open a puzzle of different kinds of trucks
I know Trev is down, thinking chemo really sucks.

"So what will you do if you lose your hair?"
I ask the question, just going right there.

He says, "I guess it's okay, but my head will get cold,
And, I like my hair. I don't want to look old."

I chuckle and punch in a puzzle piece that is blue,
"If you lose your hair, I'll shave mine off too."

I feel like I no longer have a muzzle
Keeping me from sharing my voice on life's puzzles.

In Trev's Room at Atlanta Children's Hospital
SATURDAY, APRIL 13

HOSPITALS

Nobody tells you
How noisy it is
In a hospital room.

It's something you experience
If you spend the night there.

"Time to check
Your vital signs, Trevor,"
Wanda, the night nurse says
Every hour on the hour.

And doctors?

Why do they come for their
Patient conferences before 8:00 a.m.?

And the beeps continue
Intermittent,
At different pitches,
And varying lengths,

Each sound signifying
Another breath taken
Another beat of the heart
Another of life's precious minutes consumed.

In Trev's Room at Atlanta Children's Hospital
SUNDAY, APRIL 14

PARENTS AT . . . PEACE?
(Lots of R- words in this one)

A Refreshed Mom,
And a Relaxed Dad
Arrive around 8:15 a.m.

I'm actually glad to see them.
Relieved?

Yes, I'm happy to step up,
But also Ready to Relinquish the
Responsibilities I had for just one day.

I gain a bit of appreciation
For parenting,
Caring,
Feeding,
Clothing,
And Rearing
Young
Human
Beings.

I tell them what the doctor said.
Trev seems to be "holding his own."
Chemo begins tomorrow.

Mom continues working on the puzzle
With Trev
Dad asks if I want to go with him
To get a snack.

"Sure," I say,
Realizing just how hungry
I am
For food, yes,
But also, for time with my father.

In the café at Atlanta Children's Hospital
SUNDAY, APRIL 14

THE CAFÉ WITH MY FATHER

It's like a large Starbucks,
But it has more options,
Like pasta and self-serve fountain drinks.

I order a hot chocolate
And a ham and cheese biscuit.
Dad gets a coffee-black-no cream, no sugar,
And a blueberry muffin.

We sit near the entrance
Hospital staff members
Come in and out.

"What's this I hear about
Plagiarism?" he asks.

Did he just find out about all this?

Dad impales his muffin
With his plastic knife.
That muffin is probably grateful
He's using plasticware.
I would be.

I decide to play with him . . . a little.
"I don't know. What did you hear?"

"A state test? Did you access
AI or something?" he asks.

I've taken three bites of
My biscuit, but suddenly
I'm not hungry anymore.

"Do you really think I would
Do that, Dad?"

"No, I don't. But the evidence
Your principal mentioned to us
Is pretty convincing.
She said she'd run your essay
Through three or four
Plagiarism checkers," he said.
I try to change lenses,
Look at the situation
From his perspective,
Try to
Empathize
As he continues to
Emphasize
That P word.

So funny!
A "P" using the "P" word
That has
Redefined
the last week
Of. My. Life.

"I didn't cheat.
I actually like writing essays," I say.

He's compassionate all of a sudden.
"No, Bloom. I'm sorry.
I didn't mean to sound accusatory."
Now he pokes his fork into his muffin.
"I think it's possible
Someone tampered
With your essay,
Got AI to write it."

He finishes his muffin.

"I think your Mom
Has the proof."

I honestly don't know
What to say
But I feel hungry again,
Ravenous, actually.

So, I take another bite
Of my biscuit
And let the knowledge
That my dad believes me
Wash over me
Like a cleansing shower.

At Red Hills High School, Atlanta, Georgia
Monday, April 15

MONDAY AT SCHOOL

Returning from vacations
When I was little,
Our house always seemed different,
Newer,
More colorful,
Fresher,
As if it missed us
While we were away,
And it wanted us to feel welcome
When we returned home.

I feel the same way today
Here at school.

I notice the robin's egg blue paint
On the walls of my math classroom.

The morning announcements seem
Funnier, more informative.
Did they always read
The lunch menu that way?
And play music in the background?

Even when I saw Dr. Dey
In the hallway,
She seemed to have a genuine smile
On her face.

Was I wrong about her?

In English class,
Mr. Robertson calls me to his desk.
"They're going to publish your poem, Bloom.
The one about Truth.
It won first place!
Please consider submitting more of your work," he says.

I breathe.

"Oh, and . . . " he continues.
"Next year, we're adding a
Creative Writing class.
I'd love for you to be in it."

The bell rings.

I head to my seat,
Which looks shinier, cleaner somehow.

Maya taps me on the shoulder.

I say hi.

"What's up?" she asks.

I think over the last week
Of my life . . .
Mildred.
Harold.
Albert Williams.
Gran.
And last but not least . . . Toby
And all the writing we did.

"Nothin' much," I say.

Mr. Robertson gives us our
Journal prompt for the day.

"Take fifteen minutes and write
About a change you've recently undergone
Or a change you've recently made
In your life."

Seriously?

I start writing
Immediately.

At Red Hills High School, Atlanta, Georgia
Monday, April 15

MORNING PAGES

After we finish our journals,
Mr. Robertson shows us a book called
"The Artist's Way" by Julia Cameron.

He tells us about morning pages.

At first, I think they are pages for mourning
The sad things in life,
Which I can so do!
But then, Mr. Robertson reads this ...
"Morning pages are three pages of
Longhand, stream of consciousness writing,
Done first thing in the morning.
There is no wrong way to do Morning Pages.
They are not high art. They are not even 'writing.'
They are about anything and everything that crosses your mind,
And they are for your eyes only.
Morning Pages provoke, clarify, comfort, cajole, prioritize, and
Synchronize the day at hand.
Do not overthink Morning Pages:
Just put three pages of anything on the page ...
And then do three more pages tomorrow."

Then, Mr. Robertson assigns us
Morning pages for a whole week!

Whoa, dude!
You said the Creative Writing class
Started
Next
Year!

At Red Hills High School, Atlanta, Georgia
Monday, April 15

CALLED OUT OF BIOLOGY

I've never liked missing school
Because you get
So. Much. Makeup. Work.

One time when I was in third grade,
My dad took us on a surprise trip
To Disneyworld.

I missed three days of school,
But it seemed like I had six days' worth
Of makeup work.

But so far today, all is well.
Seems like they didn't do a lot
At school last week.

Mrs. Chen, my biology teacher,
Hands me an office slip.
I'm to report to Dr. Dey
Immediately.

I already finished my notes for Chapter 23,
So, I turn them in
On my way out of the classroom.

At Red Hills High School, Atlanta, Georgia
MONDAY, APRIL 15

DR. DEY'S CONFERENCE ROOM

Mom
And Dad(?),
Are already seated.
Mom smiles at me.
I notice the tiny line
Between her brows
Has disappeared.

Ms. Kelly, the school guidance counselor,
Is also there.

"Hi," I say,
And I sit beside Dad.

The door opens
And Dr. Dey enters
Along with Mr. Hayes,
One of our assistant principals.

Dr. Dey wears a gold blouse
And a bronze skirt,
More shades of yellow.

"Good afternoon, everyone," she says.
"Thank you for coming.
We are here for an update

On the Chloe Howard case.
Mr. Hayes,
Please begin," she says.

Mr. Hayes opens a file,
And reads a paper he finds there.
"Chloe Howard was charged
With plagiarism on a state writing test.

"She was given out of school suspension
For one week.
Her test was also invalidated.
The student's mother asked if
Chloe could do community service
In a literacy program for the elderly
In Daytona Beach, Florida.
Dr. Dey, principal, approved
The request.
Chloe Howard returned to school
Today."

He looks at me.

Then, Dr. Dey speaks.

"Chloe, we would like to hear from you.
Please tell us about your community service
At . . . ," she glances at her paperwork.
"Creekside Retirement Home
In Daytona Beach, Florida."

At Red Hills High School, Atlanta, Georgia
Monday, April 15

USING MY VOICE

I didn't know I'd be doing this
Today,
But, I feel more me . . . more accepted,
Than I did
A week ago.

I look around the table,
At each person,
Then, I begin.
"I left this school
Seven days ago,
Anxious about so many things,
That would have caused me to crawl
Under my bed for decades.
The thought of sharing my voice with others
Terrified me.
But I return today,
Changed.
My eyes have been opened
Both literally and figuratively
To the Truth
Around me.

"Dr. Dey, I want to thank you
For the opportunity to spend a week
Meeting Harold, a Vietnam Veteran,
And Mildred, the retired nurse, and
So many other people.

The room is quiet,
Have I caused a silent riot?

"The experience
Gave me new lenses
To view the world."

I remember I'm supposed to meet
District requirements,
And I add, "Oh, and my grandmother signed
All the paperwork.
She's mailing it to you."

At Red Hills High School, Atlanta, Georgia
Monday, April 15

DR. DEY

She nods
While I speak.
She also writes things down
On a
Yellow
pad of paper.

"Chloe, you have an outstanding
Academic record,
And
Congratulations
On winning the national writing contest."

She looks up and
Pauses.

Then, she speaks again.

"There are three matters
I want to discuss with you."

She opens a folder.

"The first is from
Our school district's
Information Technology Department."

It says, "After completing
Extensive research in
The matter of Student #20865425's
State writing test,
We find that the student's original essay
Resulted in zero plagiarism detected."

Mr. Hayes
Looks like he
Drank lemonade
Without sugar.

"Second," Dr. Dey says,
Pulling out a journal.
Wait! No! That's my old composition book!
From middle school?!?!

Oh, no, no, no!

"Your mother submitted
This journal to me
A few weeks ago as evidence."

"She marked a few pages.
I believe you began this journal
When you were in middle school?"

I see thin pink sticky note strips
On a few of the pages.

Dr. Dey opens to the
First sticky note and reads . . .

"I've been thinking lately
About book characters
Who might have anxiety . . .
Like Jonas in 'The Giver,'
Or Odysseus, trying to get
Home to Penelope."

I cringe,
My face reddens.
I'm relieved when Dr. Dey
Stops reading.

She
Pauses
Again,
Starts to hand my journal back to
My mom, but then she
Keeps it.

"Third," Dr. Dey continues,
"While it looks as though
You did not plagiarize,
We must still await a final decision
From our school district's
Office of Student Discipline.
Of course, this journal will be
Kept as evidence for one year.
Then, it will be returned to you."

"On behalf of our school
And our school district
Please know, we are making
Every effort to resolve this . . . "

She shoots a look
At Mr. Hayes.

" . . . potential misunderstanding."

Dr. Dey closes the folder
And looks at me
And says,
"We're very proud of you, Chloe.
Keep up the great work."

Then, she
Pauses
Yet again and says,
In a higher-pitched voice,
"You know, I did some
Writing in my youth.
Poems and songs and such.
I was pretty good,"
She waits,
"Never as good as you,
Of course."

She laughs,
But no one else does.

I leave the conference room,
Wondering if I'm charged
Or cleared.

Her language is
So indirect,
Insulated,
Protected.

Oh, Truth?
Where are you?

At Red Hills High School, Atlanta, Georgia
Monday, April 15

BACK IN BIOLOGY CLASS

Only ten minutes left
In class.

Then, afternoon dismissal.

So,
I
Go
Back to biology,
And pick up my backpack.

I show Mrs. Chen
my pass. It's just a slip of paper,
But it allows me to go home early
With my mom
Since she was already here at school
For the conference.

"Proud of you, Bloom," Mrs. Chen says
With a smile.

She knows?

I feel like I got a pass
In that meeting.

Not one made of paper,
But a pass of acknowledgement
Of being seen,
Of being listened to,
Of
Being
Relieved
From the burden of false guilt

This pass is not made of paper,
It's clear, liquid Truth.

In the Howard mini-van
Monday, April 15

DRIVING HOME

I want to thank
My mom,
Let her know
How
Grateful
I
Am

For her just being herself.

"Where'd you find my journal?"
Is all I manage to utter

Before

She pulls into the parking lot
At Starbucks.

Really?

My mom?

I mean, I know she loves coffee and all,
But she's a DIY Coffee Queen.

"What's the drink called?
A Cookie Mocha?" she asks.

Who Is This Woman?

From Bloom's Blue Journal
Monday, April 15

CHANGES

We wrote about changes
In Mr. Robertson's class
Today.

But I want to write more.

I know the stereotypes about change . . .
It's hard.
    It's inevitable.
        The more things change, the more things stay the same.

But I never expected
To shed the fear
Aimed like a spear
Ready to sear
Everything I have loved and wanted.

Everything
        Is
                Different
                          Now.

And, I don't ever
Want to be accused
Of *plagiarism* again,
But
I'm
Actually
Glad
It
Happened
Because
It
Changed me for the better.

At Red Hills High School, Atlanta, Georgia
Tuesday, April 16

ANOTHER OFFICE CONFERENCE?

An office aide enters Mr. Dal Porto's Geometry classroom,
Carrying another slip of paper.

The guesses begin.
Who's in trouble?
Who's going home?

Mr. Dal Porto calls my name,
And holds up the slip
Right in the middle
Of his review of
Pythagoras and his theorem.

When will this end?

I walk to the office.
Dr. Dey stands at her door.
When she sees me,
She motions me into
The conference room.

I expect to see the whole crew
Assembled again,
But I see only . . .

Maya!

Two moist stripes
On her cheeks
Inform me
She's been crying.

The door closes.

Dr. Dey, wearing shades of gray and black
(Could this be a sign of things to come)?
Sits at the head of the table.

I sit.

"Chloe, we have had
Some new information
Surface in your
Plagiarism case."

The serpent of anxiety
Swirls in my stomach.

You know Maya Cross, I'm sure."

I nod,
Somewhat perplexed.

Maya wipes her face
With a tissue.

"She has some information
To share with you," Dr. Dey adds.

At Red Hills High School, Atlanta, Georgia
Tuesday, April 16

MAYA'S TRUTH

"Bloom . . . ," Maya says, "I've always been jealous
Of your creativity and its freshness.

"In sixth grade, you had the best idea
For our mythology project, the monologue from Hydra.

"After an enemy severed one of his heads,
He spoke and the words he said

"Worked so well, our teacher called us superstars
She used our project in some education webinar.

"But I knew what was true,
The ideas and concept came from you.

"I think back on Hydra, that nine-headed snake,
And remember how much fun he was to make.

"I guess my envy just grew
And it seemed success always found . . . you,
Never me.

"So, the day of the writing test
I figured I'd try my best
To bring you
D
O
W
N
A little.

"I used AI to write an essay.
Used your login, and I did betray
You."

Maya grabs another tissue.

"I gave you the shaft
By replacing your original draft
With one I had AI craft."

"And, I'm soooo sorry!"

Dr. Dey is strangely silent
In this awkward moment.

Then she says, "I need to call all involved,
Including the Georgia Department of Education,
To tell them this is resolved.

"You two, please return to your classes.
Here are your hall passes."

Maya and I walk down the hall
But, I'm not under a pall.

Instead, I have a new perspective
Even though Maya was quite deceptive.

At the Atlanta Children's Hospital
Tuesday, April 16

GRAN IS HERE!

I walk into Trev's hospital room.
He's sleeping,
Drooling a little on Jeffy the Giraffe.

"There you are!" Gran says.
She walks my way.
Her arms seeking to hug me.

I don't resist.

"Doing okay?"
I nod.

"We really miss you in Daytona!"

"How's Henry and Mildred,
And Toby?" I ask.
"Everyone still writing?"

My heartbeat actually quickens
As I ask this question.

"Yes, and they're doing so well.
Toby and his classmates come in twice
A week.

And, he's doing a wonderful job
Leading the writing,
Although I think he misses you."

Trev stirs in his bed,
But remains asleep.

"How is Trev?" I ask.

"The doctor said he did well,
But we need to wait a few days
To see how he reacts," Gran says.

"I won a writing contest!" I tell her.
Her hug almost smothers me!

At Red Hills High School, Atlanta, Georgia
Tuesday, April 16

OUTSIDE DR. DEY'S OFFICE

I asked Mr. Robertson
If I could come to
Dr. Dey's office during his class.

I want to ask her something.

Right now, I'm seated
In the school's main office.
Every few minutes, there's a loud buzz
At the door.

Someone wants to come in.

I wait on Dr. Dey.
Her office door is closed.

Mrs. Chen walks by and greets me.

An office aide, an eleventh grader maybe,
Works on his calculus homework at a nearby desk.

I doodle in my new, lace-covered journal.

The door opens . . .

Dr. Dey walks out with
Two men in suits and ties,
Carrying laptop cases.

The same two Ties who were with her during the test?
That seems so long ago.

I can't tell.

She sees me,
Says goodbye to the Ties,
And walks toward me.

I stand.

"Chloe," she says, her lips straining into a smile.
"Everything okay?"
I nod and smile.

"Just wondered if I could
Ask you a question
About this summer."

Dr. Dey eyes her assistant and then asks her,
"When's my next appointment?"

"Not for another half hour,"
The lady responds.

Dr. Dey walks into her office.

Am I supposed to follow her?

"Come on in, Chloe," she says.

I enter her office.
She sits behind her desk,
Puts on her glasses,
And focuses on her computer.

I sit across from her,
And open my journal to calm down
My rapid heartbeat.

"Yes?"

"Um, Dr. Dey? I just wondered
If I could go back... you know,
Continue the program in Daytona this summer.
Like officially?
My dad can fly me down there and all,
But I wanted to check on earning volunteer hours
And all that.
My grandma told me
I might get Independent Study
Credit for it."

"The Age to Page Program?" she asks,
Still looking at her screen.
"You enjoyed your week down there, didn't you?"

"I did. It was really fun
Watching the older people
Share their memories and stuff," I say.

"Honestly, I think Ms. Kelly,
Your guidance counselor, is the one
To ask about this," she says.

Dr. Dey takes off her glasses,
Then looks right at me.

"But I'll approve it,
Of course.
We must keep our
Creatives
Creating,
Mustn't we?"

*She laughs after she says this,
But it's not funny.*

"So, I?"

"Get the paperwork from
Guidance," she says.
"Fill it out,
Bring it to me.
I'll sign it."

*I already have the paperwork.
I hand it to her.*

"Thanks, Dr. Dey."

She puts on her glasses,
Looks at the forms
Then looks at her computer screen again.

Is that my cue to exit?

I think it is, but I decide
To ask the question
I've been wanting to ask.

"Aren't you a writer, Dr. Dey?"

Her face stiffens,
But she still looks at the screen.

"Me?
I did some writing
Back in my day.
Nothing like yours,
Chloe."

She reaches for a book
In a bookshelf
Behind her desk.

"This is my copy of
'The Odyssey' from high school," she says.

She pauses.

"Take a look at my notes
From all those years ago.
Let me know what you think."

Then, she smiles and silently
Dismisses me.

Bloom's home
TUESDAY, APRIL 16

WHO ARE THESE PEOPLE?

This literally sounds like a song,
But my parents are actually getting along.

They don't even seem to argue
Instead, unity is in view.

Is it because of Trev's disease
This brand-new sense of peace?

We also bit the bullet,
And now, we're on a budget.

No more Mocha Cookie Crumbles for a while.

From Bloom's Blue Journal
WEDNESDAY, APRIL 17

THE YO-YO DIARIES PART 6: TREV'S CONDITION

Trev's condition has gotten worse
At least, he's not in a hearse.

I try to see him every day after school
But sometimes, reality is too cruel.

I call him every night
It's the thing to do; it is right.

I pray he doesn't get worse or die
I need to write about this, and cry.

His chemo doesn't seem to be working,
I have a suspicion lurking.

From Bloom's Blue Journal

THURSDAY, APRIL 18—EARLY MORNING

MORNING PAGES

I kinda like writing these morning pages. Feels like I can release the clutter in my mind here.

Mr. Robertson says you just write about anything. So, I'll write about jealousy.

One time in second grade I was jealous of a kid named Nick because he got this board with real electrical circuits he could play with. It lit up and everything! I absolutely pressured my mom using my best kid tactics. She eventually caved in and bought one for me. The sad thing is, I think I played with it only two or three times.

Anyway, I don't think anyone has ever been jealous of me, except for Maya. There is truly nothing to be jealous of in my life, but I guess we all have different perspectives.

I have to give it to Maya, though. Her plan was slick. She turned on her phone's hotspot that day in the cafeteria before she carried her backpack out of the room. Then, she opened a browser and asked AI write an essay on the prompt.

She already knew my login and password, so she logged on as me, deleted my work, and pasted in the partial AI essay. Kinda diabolical if you really think about it.

Luckily, the investigators knew how to go through saved data and find the . . . truth. The essay I wrote was never really deleted.

But, unluckily, they never showed Mom or Dad or me the essay Maya uploaded to my testing portal. If they had, I wouldn't have had to go through any of this.

I wonder about these high stakes tests sometimes. Different topic for a different day.

Wait, I think I smell bacon. I love it when my dad cooks breakfast!

I think bacon is worth pausing these pages.

Red Hills High School, Atlanta, Georgia—One month later
THURSDAY, MAY 23

LAST WEEK OF SCHOOL

I hate starting school in August
Until we get out in May!

Three more days of school,
Then I fly to Daytona
For four days.

Dr. Dey signed my forms
And deliver them
To me
Personally
In Mrs. Chen's room.

On airplane flying to Daytona
SATURDAY, MAY 25

AIRBORNE

The flight is short,
But it takes me
Away
    From
        This
            Year.

I stayed late in Trev's hospital room
Last night.
Read him four stories.

We snuggled in his bed,
Trev, Jeffy, and me.
The doctor's think
He may be doing a little better.

I have a book Mr. Robertson recommended
With me here on the plane.
It's a book of poems by Ogden Nash.

Ogden Nash was apparently
Known for witty
And humorous verse
Such as ...
"Celery raw, develops the jaw,
But celery stewed, is more quietly chewed."

Okay, I like this guy.
He's clever with his words.
He's written poems about leopards,
Cows, flies, and pigs.
He even has a poem
About an octopus.
But that's not all.
I actually laugh out loud
Reading the poems on the plane.

Chuckles at 25,000 feet?

We should definitely read these poems
At Age to Page.

At the Daytona International Airport
SATURDAY, MAY 25

REPEAT

I walk the sky bridge
Expecting to see Gran
At the end.

But, the first person I see
Is a tall,
African American
Male.

Toby!

I run and hug him.

"Whoa, what's this?" he asks
Taking Nash from my hands.
"Reading light verse, are we?"
He jokes.

Gran walks over
Holding a cardboard drink carrier
Full of mocha cookie crumbles
From Starbucks.

"I'm hooked," she says.

"Done with school?" I ask Toby.

"Nah, one more week," he says.
"But, I'll be at the facility
Tomorrow."

We don't need to go to baggage claim
Because I only have a carry-on.

"Been writing?" he asks.

I nod.

"I brought three journals
Full of stuff," I say.

"Me, too!" Gran says.
"Let's sit over here."

We sit in the food court
At a white plastic table
And my joy spills over,
Just like the whipped cream
From my mocha cookie crumble.

At the Daytona International Airport
SATURDAY, MAY 25

JOY!

I'm literally shaking
As I open my blue journal.

I have
So
Much
To
Say
And share.

I am right where I want to be,
Sharing words,
Using my voice.

I read them my poem
About change

Because I've changed
So much
Seeing more of the Truth
In so many situations.

I see the future
As a place
To change more.

At the Daytona International Airport
Saturday, May 25

GRAN'S POEM

I knew Gran loved reading
But I didn't know she could
Write like that!

Here's part of what she read to us . . .

Time is a foggy landscape,
Hosting human feet
From generation to generation
From iteration to celebration
Of life's
Peace and strife.
Time is one definition of life.

She sips her mocha cookie crumble
Then, she says
"Let's hear something from Toby!"

Toby blushes,
I think.

At the Daytona International Airport
S̴aturday, May 25

TOBY'S POEM

He pulls out his phone,
Opens his notes app,
And writing's gales come again.

Hurricanes
Wind and rain
Washing away spots
From my stained, stormy soul.
The rage in the sky,
Makes me ask why
I'm here
In this cultural moment
Where questions of identity
Threaten to suffocate me
Like the wind and rain
Of a hurricane.
And yet,
I know I can rest
In the Eye
Where there's Peace,
Beauty,
Truth,
And my true identity,
Which starts with I.

At Gran's Condo
SATURDAY, MAY 25

RESTFUL

I walk into
Grandpa's library,
Kneel down to my shelf,
And pull out his copy of
The Odyssey
I can't wait to compare it
To Dr. Dey's copy
Which I brought with me.

As I open Grandpa's book,
I realize
I've been on an odyssey
Of my own.

Book in hand,
I recline on the chaise.

I open to Book 12,
Where Odysseus
Sails between
Scylla and Charybdis,
Those rocky obstacles.

I've had obstacles of my own
This year,
But I can't wait
To go to Gran's facility
Tomorrow
And share my words,
My voice
With my friends there.

At Gran's condo
SATURDAY, MAY 25

A VISIT FROM CALLIE

Of course, I was hoping
I might see her
Somehow,
But when I open
Dr. Dey's copy of
The Odyssey,
And I see her notes
In the margins
In red ink,
I know she's here.

She's been in both books!

"Callie?" I say.

"I'm here, Bloom.
Always with you
In your imagination," she says to me.

"I was cleared
Of all charges," I say
Aloud in Grandpa's library.

"Keep reading, keep thinking,
Keep writing,
And above all,
Keep sharing your voice.
The world needs to hear you," she says.

I smile and say,
"I'm putting together
A poetry collection . . .
About . . . well, about everything
That's happened this year,
From Trev to the plagiarism charge
To my dad . . . ," I stop.
I'm close to tears.
Then, I say,
"I'll dedicate it to you,
And to Grandpa."

"The world needs to hear
What you have to say," she says again.
And then, I close the book
And fall asleep on the chaise.

Creekside Retirement Home—Meeting Room
Monday, May 27

REUNION

There aren't as many
Old folks in attendance today,
But I see Henry,
And Mildred,
And Albert.

We exchange hugs
And small talk,
Except now, I don't mind it.
Somehow, it connects us
Even more.

Mildred asks,
"What have you been writing?"

"I'm actually putting together
A poetry collection," I reply.

She smiles and says,
"Tell me the minute
It's published.
I'm buying copies
For all ten of my grandchildren.

I turn red.

Henry tells me he's writing a book
About his time in Vietnam.

Toby enters a few minutes later.
He nods his head at me
Then speaks with Albert.

Gran asks me to lead a writing exercise.

I go to the podium
And ask everyone to write
About circles.
"Circles?" Mildred asks.

"Circles in life," I respond.
"Rings we wear,
Things we share,
Moments when we realize
We've come full circle."

The room quiets
As everyone
Writes.

Creekside Retirement Home—Meeting Room
Monday, May 27

MY POEM: CIRCLES

Back in the fall
I was in a pall,
Not really living
Definitely not giving
Of myself.

Instead, I had serious anxiety
Suffering like many in this society
Then, one of the worst things ever
Happened and threatened to sever
Me from myself.

A false and mean accusation
Almost took me out of circulation
Virtually stopped me from writing
And started the fighting
Between my speaking and my silence.

My punishment became a gift
That caused within me a shift
And I realized my writing
Could serve as my way of righting
Wrongs I've seen done to myself and others.

And so, my circle is complete
I will no longer retreat
After seeking the Truth
At this time, in my youth
I must share it with the world.

The future I face is uncertain
But I know I can open the curtain
By writing and learning
Finding and yearning
To follow the Truth.

I don't know what will happen with my brother,
Or with my father and my mother.
But as a family, we are united
Truth has been invited
Into our home and family.

Creekside Retirement Home—Meeting Room
Tuesday, May 28

PUBLISHED!

(My poem's on page 28)

It's a booklet
With a cover
That has a cool
"Age to Page" logo
On it,
Thanks to Toby
And his handy-dandy laptop.

I flip through it.

It smells fresh and flourishing
And it's full of life.

It's 101 pages
Of words,
Thoughts,
Voices,
Fears,
Hope,
Change,

And

Truth!

I turn to page twenty eight.
That's my page.

From the Age to Page booklet
PAGE 28

OPPOSITES ATTRACT?
by Bloom Howard

Big, Small?
Short, Tall?

Polka Dot or Plaid?
Opposing forces don't make me mad.
That said,

Dim, Bright,
Black, White,
Darkness, Light,
Opposites seem to be misunderstood
In their universal brotherhood.

But Darkness will never overcome Light,
Even though it puts up a fight.
It's going to be alright.

Opposites attract,
But they are also abstract,
And Light can refract
In so many directions,
And answer so many of my questions.

From Bloom's Blue Journal
Friday, August 2

A NEW YEAR

I've always liked
Starting over in January
And
In August.

You get two chances
To get it right.

I start tenth grade
In about a week.
I'm taking
Honors classes
And
Mr. Robertson's
Creative Writing Class!

Trev stayed in the hospital
Until the end of June.
Then, he came home.
He starts his next round
Of Chemo tomorrow.

He's holding on.

When I think back over what's happened,
I wonder why Maya did what she did.
Even if she was jealous of me,
Why did she try to bring me
D
o
w
n?

I may not ever know.

I started going to youth group meetings
Here in Atlanta.
I've met some really nice friends.

Tessa told me I was through with therapy
Back in July.
But, she told me
I had to keep journaling
And
Yo-yo-ing

Fine by me!

Oh, and I forgot to tell you,
I'm doing an independent study next year.
I'll go to Gran's four times
To help her with Age to Page.
Dr. Dey even mentioned
Starting a similar program
Here in Atlanta.

The first visit is near the end of the month.
I'll get to watch my first NASCAR race!
Gran's already bought tickets!

In any case, I hope I see Callie
and Toby again!

I'm literally a
Different
Person
From who I was last year.

I'm proud of myself,
And I think Grandpa
would be proud of me.

Epilogue

Bloom's first place poem

TRUTH SEEKER

Truth.
Where are you?

Many cultures and peoples
Have searched for you
In Nature,
In Holy Books,
And in Sages
Throughout the ages.

But I think you like to hide,
Never revealing where you reside.

I think you wish to be sought
By those who exercise thought.

Do we decide who and what you are?
As we routinely wish upon a star?

I want to learn
As I continually yearn

To know What and Who you are.

Truth,
Please cease
To be a mystery
And show yourself
At this moment in history.

I am a seeker.
Must I be meeker
Or become weaker
In my search for You?

Or will you share a revelation
With me and my generation?

I hope so.

Journal Prompts Recommended by Bloom

1. Write about your relationship with Truth. How do you define it? Where do you find it?
2. Have you ever had a close relative get sick or hospitalized? Write about your feelings during that time.
3. Do you have favorite children's books? If so, what are they? Write about one or two of them here. Why were they your favorites?
4. Did you make up stories as a child? If so, what or who were they about?
5. Have you ever played with a yo-yo? If so, describe the experience. If not, did you have other toys you played with as a child?
6. Anxiety is real. What makes you feel anxious or worried in your current day-to-day life? Sometimes, just writing about it helps!
7. Have you ever been jealous of someone? How did you work through your feelings?
8. Have you ever been on an odyssey? Were there obstacles you overcame along the way?
9. What are your thoughts about my story? Did you like it? Did you relate to any of it?
10. If you're a student, you've probably taken a lot of tests. How do you feel about the testing environment these days? Do you agree or disagree with Bloom's conclusions about standardized testing?

www.ingramcontent.com/pod-product-compliance
Lightning Source LLC
Chambersburg PA
CBHW060556230426
43670CB00011B/1847